THE GARDEN SUNFLOWER QUILT

THE GARDEN SUNFLOWER QUILT

Design by Cheryl Benner
Text by Rachel T. Pellman

Good Books

Intercourse, PA 17534

The Garden Sunflower Quilt pattern was designed exclusively for Turkey Hill Dairy to commemorate the 10th Anniversary of the Ice Cream Festival, held on Sunday, July 17, 1994, in Lancaster, Pennsylvania. Ice cream lovers throughout Pennsylvania and neighboring states attend this annual event held in Lancaster Square. The Festival is underwritten by Turkey Hill Dairy, and all its proceeds, including the quilt raffle, are donated to the Library System of Lancaster County to purchase children's books. We're delighted that this pattern is now available through this book.

Design by Cheryl Benner
Cover and color photography by Jonathan Charles

THE COUNTRY SUNFLOWER QUILT
© 1995 by Good Books, Intercourse, PA 17534
International Standard Book Number: 1-56148-133-5
Library of Congress Catalog Card Number: 95-2504

Library of Congress Cataloging-in-Publication Data

Benner, Cheryl A., 1962-
    The garden sunflower quilt / design by Cheryl Benner ; text by Rachel T. Pellman.
        p. cm.
    ISBN 1-56148-133-5
    1. Quilting--Patterns. 2. Applique--Patterns. 3. Flowers in art.
I. Pellman, Rachel T. (Rachel Thomas) II. Title.
TT835.B355   1995
746.46--dc20   95-2504
                                                                          CIP

Table of Contents

THE GARDEN SUNFLOWER QUILT

The Garden Sunflower Quilt gathers the colors and flowers of summertime and combines them with traditional patchwork to create a warm and charming quilt design.

The quilt's center is filled with bold appliqued sunflowers, tulips, and ivy leaves, which encircle a delicately quilted watering can.

Surrounding the appliqued center are a series of pieced blocks, derived from the comforting Log Cabin patch. Each pieced block echoes the vivid colors of the appliqued flowers and enhances their place in the "garden." The pleasant contrast of patchwork and applique occurs again with sunflowers at each corner.

A unique "envelope style" pillow throw design complements the quilt's interior. Flowing ivy leaves on an inner border form a triangle around a spray of sunflowers and tulips.

More sunflowers with leaves finish the outer borders of this quilt, each cluster fitting into the curves of the softly indented edges.

Though sunflowers occur naturally only in yellow, this design can be adapted to many color preferences. Two variations appear in this book. May you be inspired and challenged to use this design to create a quilt of your own!

How to Begin

Read the following instructions thoroughly before beginning work on your quilt.

All fabrics should be washed before they are cut. This step preshrinks and also tests fabrics for colorfastness. If the fabric is not colorfast after one washing, either repeat the washings until the water remains clear, or replace the cloth with another fabric. If fabrics are wrinkled after washing and drying, iron them before using them.

Fabrics suitable for quilting are generally lightweight, tightly woven cotton and cotton/polyester blends. They should not unravel easily and should not hold excessive wrinkles when they are squeezed and released. Because of the hours of time required to make a quilt, it is worth investing in high quality fabrics.

Fabric requirements given here are for standard 45" wide fabric. If you use wider or more narrow fabrics, calculate the variations needed.

All seams are sewn using $1/4$" seam allowances. Measurements given include seam allowances, except for applique pieces (See "How to Applique," beginning on page 6.).

Fabric Requirements
for Queen-size or Double-size Quilt

Background for applique patches—$2^{1}/4$ yards
Borders and alternate blocks—$4^{3}/4$ yards
Back of quilt—$6^{3}/4$ yards
Ivy border around pillow throw triangle—$1^{1}/2$ yards
Binding—$1^{1}/4$ yards
Pieced blocks (templates given) A—$1/8$ yard; B, C—$1/4$ yard; D, E—$1/4$ yard; F, G—$3/8$ yard; H, I—$1/2$ yard (unless using leftover fabric from the border around the pillow throw for H and I)
Applique: Sunflower A petals—$1/8$ yd. each of 2 fabrics
Sunflower A centers—$1/8$ yd. each of 2 fabrics
Sunflower B petals—$1/4$ yd. each of 2 fabrics
Sunflower B centers—$1/8$ yd. each of 2 fabrics
Sunflower C petals—$1/8$ yd. each of 2 fabrics
Sunflower C centers—$1/4$ yd. each of 2 fabrics
Sunflower D petals—$1/2$ yd. each of 2 fabrics
Sunflower D centers—$1/2$ yd. each of 2 fabrics
Outer tulip—$1/8$ yd.
Tulip center—$1/8$ yd.
Pointed leaf—$5/8$ yd.
Large Ivy leaf—$1/8$ yd. of one fabric; $1/4$ yd. of a different fabric
Small Ivy leaf—$1/4$ yd. each of 2 fabrics
Bias tape for stems—7 yds.

Cutting Layout for Queen-Size or Double-Size Quilt
Finished size approximately 90" x 105"
Measurements shown here include seam allowances.

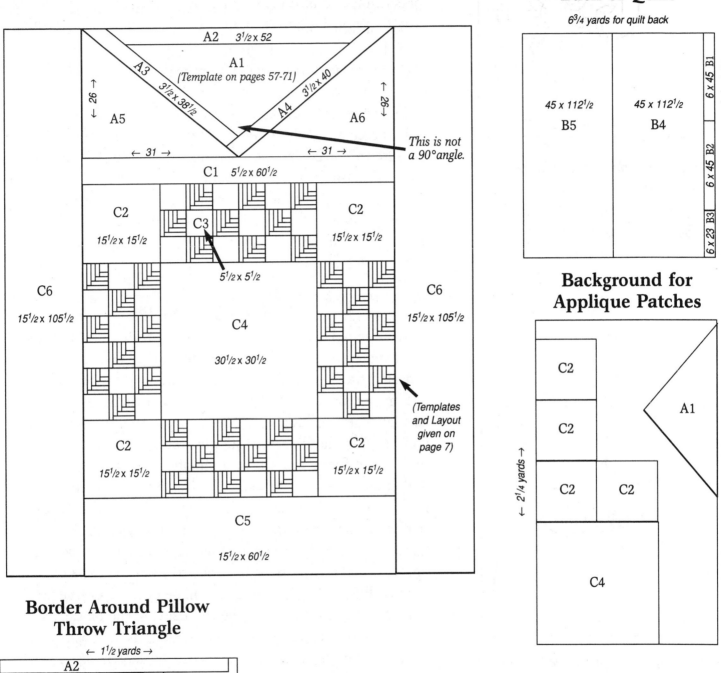

A2 3¹/₂ x 52

A1
(Template on pages 57-71)

A3 3¹/₂ x 38¹/₂

A4 3¹/₂ x 40

← 26 → **A5**   **A6** ← 26 →

This is not a 90° angle.

← 31 →   ← 31 →

C1 5¹/₂ x 60¹/₂

C2 15¹/₂ x 15¹/₂

C3 5¹/₂ x 5¹/₂

C2 15¹/₂ x 15¹/₂

C6 15¹/₂ x 105¹/₂

C4 30¹/₂ x 30¹/₂

C6 15¹/₂ x 105¹/₂

(Templates and Layout given on page 7)

C2 15¹/₂ x 15¹/₂   **C2** 15¹/₂ x 15¹/₂

C5 15¹/₂ x 60¹/₂

Back of Quilt
6³/₄ yards for quilt back

B5 45 x 112¹/₂
B4 45 x 112¹/₂
B1 6 x 45
B2 6 x 45
B3 6 x 23

Background for Applique Patches

← 2¹/₄ yards →

C2
C2
C2 **C2**
C4

A1

Border Around Pillow Throw Triangle

← 1¹/₂ yards →

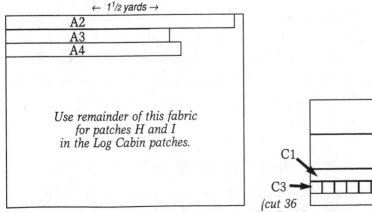

A2
A3
A4

Use remainder of this fabric for patches H and I in the Log Cabin patches.

Borders and Alternate Blocks

← 4³/₄ yards →

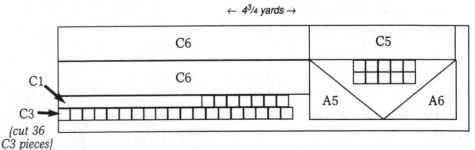

C6

C6

C1

C3
(cut 36 C3 pieces)

C5

A5   **A6**

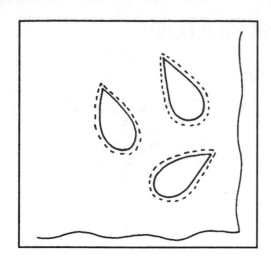

Applique templates should be traced on the right side of the fabric but spaced far enough apart so they can be cut approximately ¹/₄" outside the marked line.

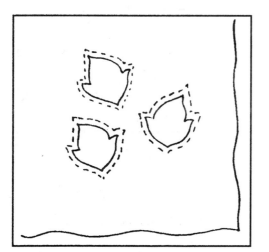

Each applique piece needs to be traced separately (rather than having the fabric doubled) so the fold line is marked on each one. However, since some of the pieces face in opposite directions, half should be traced in one direction and the other half should be traced in the opposite direction (see illustration above).

Preparing Background Fabric for Appliqueing

When you purchase fabric for the background and borders, buy the total amount you need from one bolt of fabric, if possible. This will assure that all the patches and borders will be the same shade. Dye lots can vary significantly from bolt to bolt of fabric, and those differences are emphasized when placed next to each other in a quilt top.

Cutting diagrams are shown on page 5 to make the most efficient use of fabric. Label each piece as soon as you've cut it. Mark the right and wrong sides of the fabric as well.

To indicate the placement of applique pieces on the background piece, trace the applique design lightly on the right side of the background fabric. Even though the applique pieces will be laid over these markings and stitched in place, it is important to mark these lines as lightly as possible to avoid show-through. Center the applique designs on the background sections.

Making Templates

Make templates from pattern pieces printed in this book, using material that will not wear along the edges with repeated tracing. Cardboard is suitable for pieces which you will trace only a few times. Plastic lids or the sides of plastic cartons work well for templates that you will use repeatedly. Quilt supply shops and art supply stores carry sheets of plastic that function well for template-making.

Precision begins with marking. The applique templates are given in their actual size, without seam allowances. Trace them that way. Then trace the templates on the right side of the fabric, but spaced far enough apart so that they can be cut approximately ¹/₄" outside the marked line. The traced line is the fold line, indicating the exact shape of the applique piece. Since these lines will be on the right side of the fabric and will be on the folded edge, make the markings as light as possible.

Each applique piece needs to be traced separately (rather than having the fabric doubled) so the fold line is marked on each one. However, since some of the pieces face in opposite directions, half should be traced in one direction and the other half should be traced in the opposite direction (see illustration on left).

How to Applique

Begin by appliqueing the cut-out fabric pieces, one at a time, over the placement lines drawn onto the background fabric pieces. Be alert to the sequence in which the pieces are applied, so that sections which overlay each other are done in proper order. In cases where a portion of an applique piece is covered by another, the section being covered does not need to be stitched, since it will be held in place by the stitches of the section that overlays it.

Appliqueing is not difficult, but it does require patience and precision. The best applique work has perfectly smooth curves and sharply defined points. To achieve this, make your stitches very small and tight. First, pin the piece being appliqued to the outline on the background piece. Using thread that matches the piece being applied, stitch the piece to the background section, folding the seam allowance under to the traced line on the applique piece. Fold under only a tiny section at a time.

The applique stitch is a running stitch going through the background fabric and emerging to catch only a few threads of the appliqued piece along the fold line. The needle should re-enter the background piece for the next stitch at almost the same place it emerged, creating a stitch so small that it is almost invisible along the edge of the appliqued piece. Stitches on the underside of the background fabric should be about $1/16$"-$1/8$" long.

To form sharp points, fold in one side and stitch almost to the end of the point. Fold in the opposite side to form the point and push the excess seam allowance under with the point of the needle. Stitch tightly.

To form smooth curves, clip along the curves to the fold line. Fold under while stitching, using the needle to push under the seam allowances.

Because the background section of the pillow throw is triangular and will therefore have a bias edge, it works best to assemble the pillow throw section before doing the applique to avoid stretching the bias edges. See the section "Assembling the Pillow Throw" on page 8 for instructions.

When you have completed all the applique work, you are ready to begin making the patchwork blocks.

Making the Patchwork Blocks

Templates for pieced blocks are given in this book on page 13. Each template is shown *with* $1/4$" seam allowances added.

The key to successful piecework is accuracy. Each piece must be cut with precision and sewn using accurate $1/4$" seam allowances.

See the adjoining diagram for making the blocks. It is most efficient to move from Step A to Step B for all patches, and

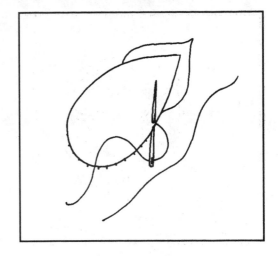

The applique stitch is a tiny, tight stitch that goes through the background fabric and emerges to catch only a few threads of the appliqued piece along the fold line.

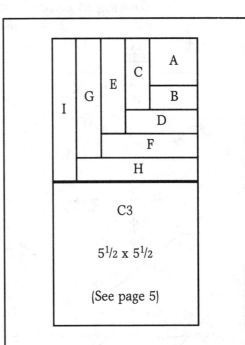

Moving in order from Step A through Step I, sew pieces together with $1/4$" seams.

Then attach the pieced block to the plain block (C3), alternating pieced and plain blocks to form rows of 6 blocks. Attach rows of 6 blocks together to form units of 3 blocks x 6 blocks (see page 9).

7

then move from Step B to Step C (and so on) for all patches, rather than assembling one block fully before moving on to the next one.

To be efficient, stack the patches next to your sewing machine and stitch them one after another without clipping the threads between each set. In the end there will be a long chain of patches which can be clipped apart as you move to the next step.

Fold all seam allowances in the same direction. When quilting the patches, quilt along the seams *away* from the seam allowances to avoid having to quilt through several thicknesses.

Assembling the Quilt Top and Back

When you have completed all the applique and patchwork, you are ready to assemble the whole quilt. See the diagrams below for instructions.

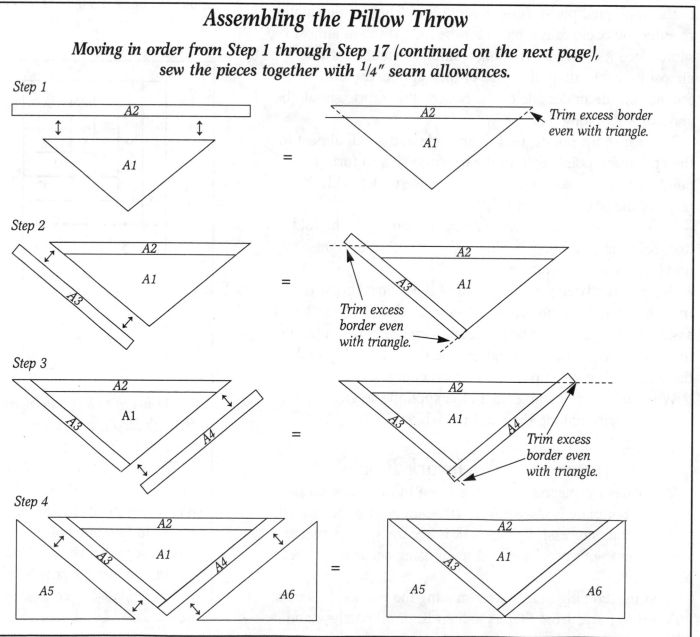

Assembling the Pillow Throw

*Moving in order from Step 1 through Step 17 (continued on the next page),
sew the pieces together with ¹/₄" seam allowances.*

Step 1

A2 A1 = A2 A1 → Trim excess border even with triangle.

Step 2

A2 A1 A3 = A2 A3 A1 Trim excess border even with triangle.

Step 3

A2 A1 A3 A4 = A2 A3 A1 A4 Trim excess border even with triangle.

Step 4

A2 A1 A3 A4 A5 A6 = A2 A3 A1 A5 A6

Assembling the Quilt Top

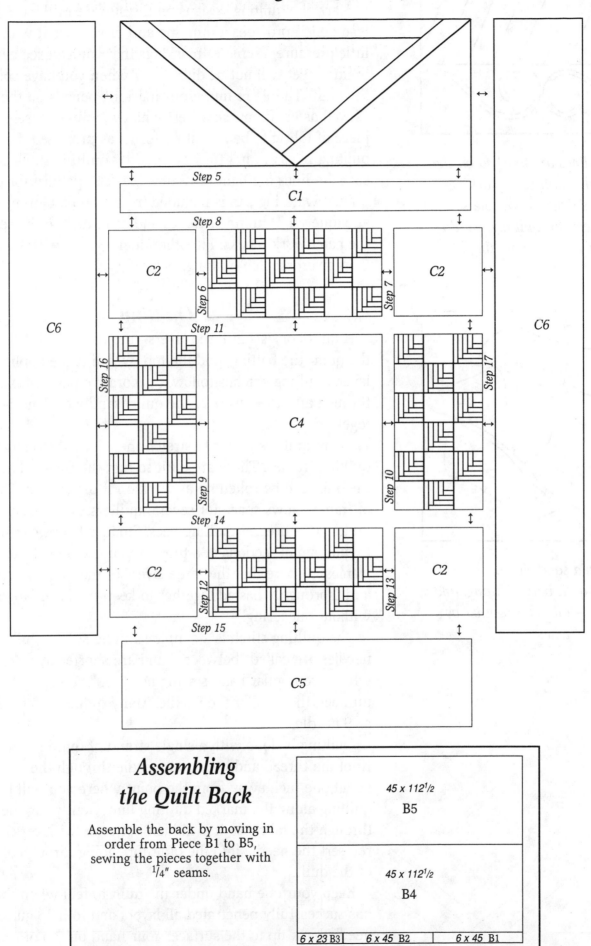

Assembling the Quilt Back

Assemble the back by moving in order from Piece B1 to B5, sewing the pieces together with 1/4" seams.

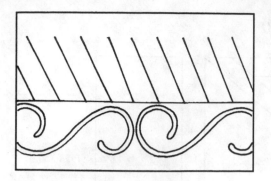

Quilting lines are marked on the surface of the quilt top. Markings should be as light as possible so they are easily seen for quilting, yet do not distract when the quilting is completed.

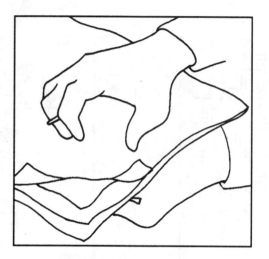

A quilt is a sandwich of three layers—the quilt back, batting, and the quilt top—all held together by the quilting stitches.

Marking Quilting Designs

Mark the quilting designs on the surface of the quilt top. A lead pencil provides a thin line and, if you use it with very little pressure, it creates markings that you can see easily for quilting, yet will not be distracting when you have completed the quilt. There are numerous marking pencils on the market, as well as chalk markers. Test whatever you choose on a scrap piece of fabric to be sure it performs as promised. Remember, quilting lines are not fully covered by quilting stitches, so be sure the lines are light or removable. The pattern for the quilted watering can is included in this book. Outline all applique with quilting stitches and quilt next to the seams of the patchwork blocks. Fill other open spaces with straight lines or crosshatch quilting.

Quilting

A quilt consists of three layers—the back or underside of the quilt, the batting, and the top, which is the appliqued layer. Quilting stitches follow a decorative pattern, piercing through all three layers of the quilt "sandwich" and holding it together.

Many quilters prefer to stretch their quilts into large quilting frames. These are built so that the finished area of the quilt can be rolled up as work on it progresses. This type of frame allows space for several quilters to work on the same quilt and is used at quilting bees. Smaller hoops can be used to quilt small sections at a time. If you use one of the smaller frames, be sure that the three layers of the quilt are stretched and thoroughly basted together to keep the layers together without puckering.

The quilting stitch is a simple running stitch. Quilting needles are called "betweens" and are shorter than "sharps," which are regular hand-sewing needles. The higher the number, the smaller the needle. Many quilters prefer a size 8 or 9 needle.

Quilting is done with a single strand of quilting thread. Knot the thread and insert the needle through the top layer, about one inch away from the point where you will begin quilting along the marked quilting line. Gently tug the knot through the fabric so it is hidden between the layers. Then reinsert the needle into the quilt top, going through all layers of the quilt.

Keep your one hand under the quilt to feel when the needle has successfully penetrated all layers and to help guide the needle back up to the surface. Your hand on top of the quilt will receive the needle and repeat the process. You can stack a series of as many as five stitches on the needle before you pull the thread through. When you are working curves, stack fewer stitches. Pull the quilting stitches taut, but not so tight as to pucker the fabric.

When you have used the entire length of thread, reinforce the stitching with a tiny backstitch. Then reinsert the needle in the top layer, push it through for a long stitch, and then pull it out and clip it.

The goal in quilting is to have straight, even stitches that are of equal length on both the top and bottom of the quilt. You will achieve this only with hours of practice.

Binding

The final stage in completing a quilt is the binding, which finishes the quilt's raw edge. When you bind the edges of a scalloped quilt, it is best to cut the binding strips on the bias. This allows more flex and stretch around curves. To cut on the bias, cut the fabric at a 45 degree angle to the straight of grain.

A double thickness of binding on the edge of the quilt gives it additional strength and durability. To create a double binding, cut the binding strips 2-2^1/$_2$" wide. Sew the strips together to form a continuous length of binding. For a scalloped-edge quilt, this length will need to equal the length of the two sides, plus the bottom edge of the quilt. The upper edge is straight.

To sew binding on a scalloped edge, baste the raw edges of the quilt together. Mark the scallops. Sew the binding along the marked edge. Trim the scallops even with the edge of the binding. Wrap the binding around to the back, enclosing the raw edges and covering the stitch line. Slipstitch in place with thread that matches the color of the binding fabric.

Displaying Quilts

Wall quilts can be hung in various ways. One is simply to tack the quilt directly to the wall. However, this is potentially damaging to both the quilt and the wall. Except for a permanent hanging, this is probably not the best way.

Another option is to hang the quilt like a painting. To do this, make a narrow sleeve from matching fabric and handsew it to the upper edge of the quilt along the back. Insert a dowel rod through the sleeve and hang the rod by wire or nylon string.

The quilt can also be hung on a frame. This method

requires Velcro or fabric to be attached to the frame itself. If you use Velcro, staple one side of it to the frame. Handsew the opposite Velcro on the edges of the quilt, then attach it carefully to the Velcro on the frame. If fabric is attached to the frame, the quilt is then handstitched to the frame itself.

Quilts can also be mounted inside Plexiglas by a professional framery. This method, often reserved for antique quilts, provides an acid-free, dirt-free and, with special Plexiglas, a sun-proof environment for your quilt.

Signing and Dating Quilts

To preserve history for future generations, sign and date the quilts you make. Include your initials and the year you made the quilt. It is customary to add this data discreetly in a corner of the quilt. You can also embroider or quilt this information among the quilting designs. Another alternative is to stitch or write the information on a separate piece of fabric and handstitch it to the back of the quilt. Whatever method you choose, this is an important part of finishing a quilt.

The Garden Sunflower Quilt Log Cabin Block Templates

[B & C are the same fabric, D & E are the same fabric, F & G are the same fabric, H & I are the same fabric.]
Seam allowance IS included on these templates.

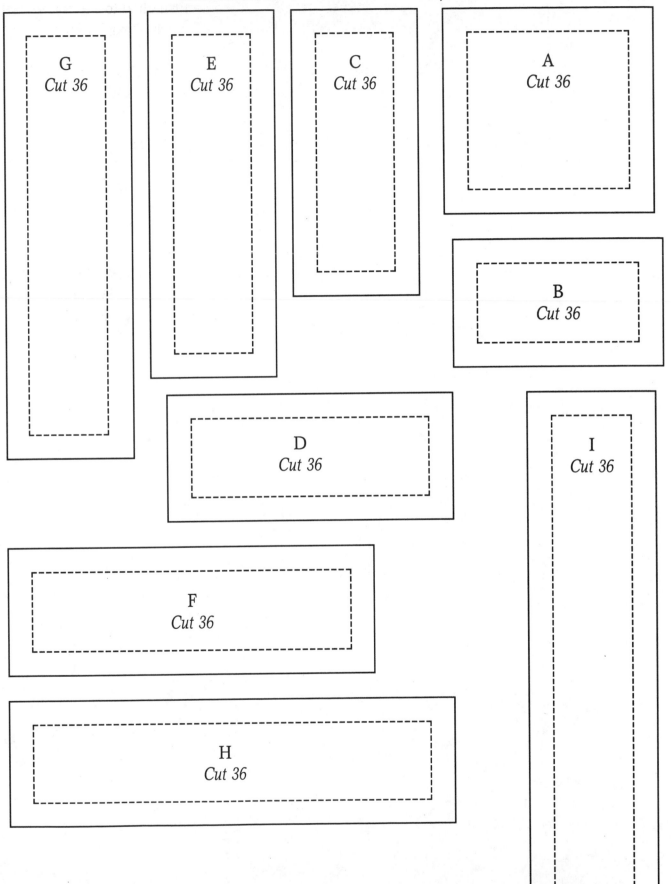

G
Cut 36

E
Cut 36

C
Cut 36

A
Cut 36

B
Cut 36

D
Cut 36

I
Cut 36

F
Cut 36

H
Cut 36

The Garden Sunflower Quilt Applique Templates

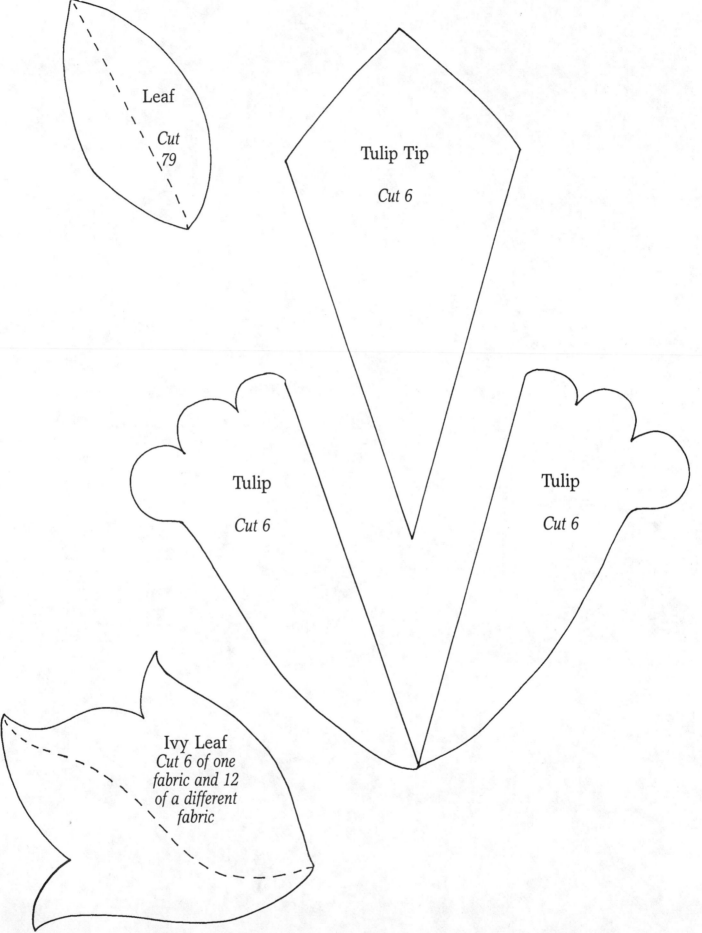

Leaf

Cut 79

Tulip Tip

Cut 6

Tulip

Cut 6

Tulip

Cut 6

Ivy Leaf
Cut 6 of one fabric and 12 of a different fabric

The Garden Sunflower Quilt Applique Templates
Sunflower Ⓐ

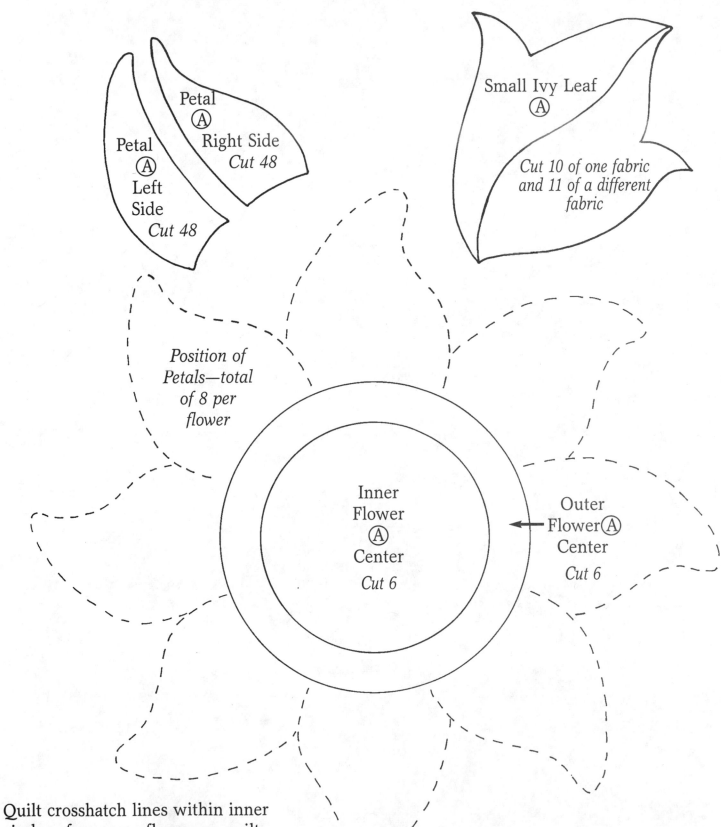

Petal Ⓐ Right Side
Cut 48

Petal Ⓐ Left Side
Cut 48

Small Ivy Leaf Ⓐ

Cut 10 of one fabric and 11 of a different fabric

Position of Petals—total of 8 per flower

Inner Flower Ⓐ Center
Cut 6

Outer Flower Ⓐ Center
Cut 6

Quilt crosshatch lines within inner circles of *every* sunflower on quilt.

Total of 6 size A Sunflowers needed.

The Garden Sunflower Quilt Applique Templates
Sunflower Ⓑ

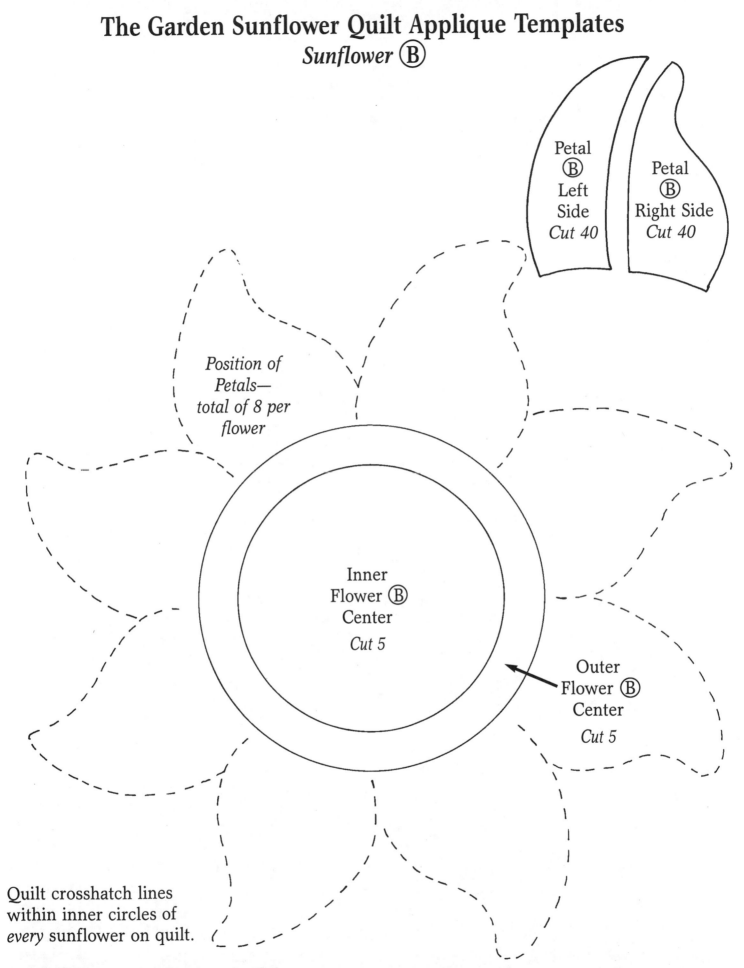

Petal
Ⓑ
Left
Side
Cut 40

Petal
Ⓑ
Right Side
Cut 40

*Position of
Petals—
total of 8 per
flower*

Inner
Flower Ⓑ
Center

Cut 5

Outer
Flower Ⓑ
Center

Cut 5

Quilt crosshatch lines
within inner circles of
every sunflower on quilt.

Total of 5 size B Sunflowers needed.

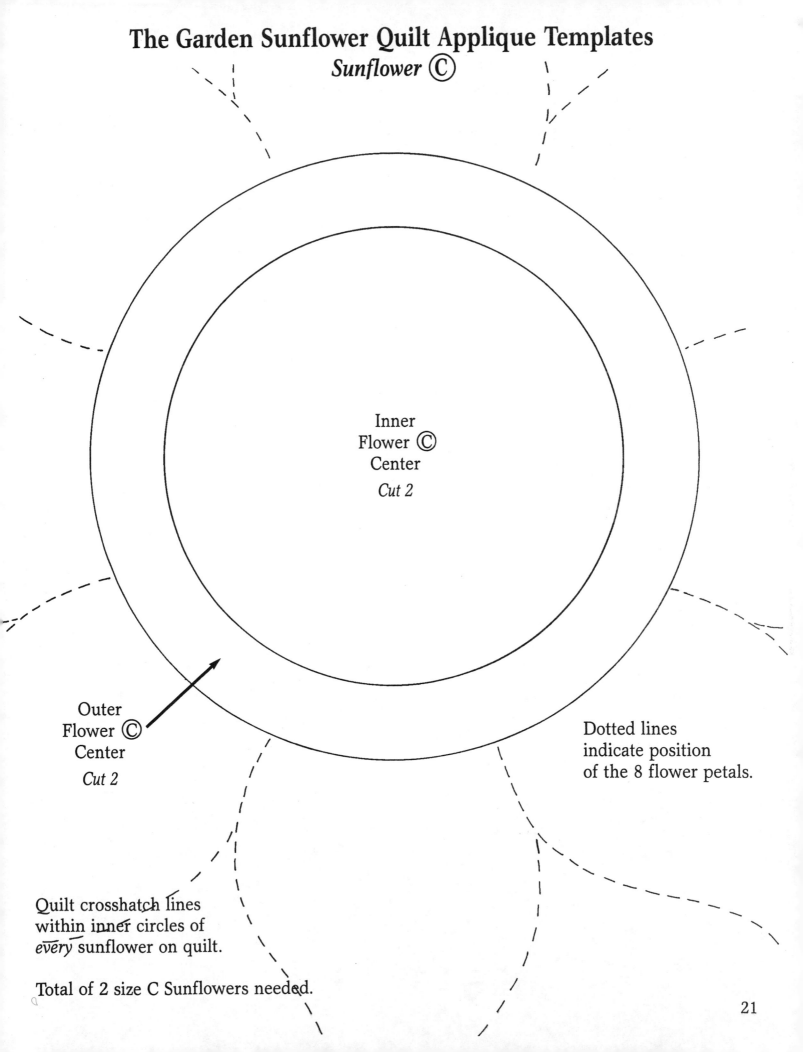

The Garden Sunflower Quilt Applique Templates
Sunflower Ⓒ

Inner
Flower Ⓒ
Center

Cut 2

Outer
Flower Ⓒ
Center

Cut 2

Dotted lines
indicate position
of the 8 flower petals.

Quilt crosshatch lines
within inner circles of
every sunflower on quilt.

Total of 2 size C Sunflowers needed.

The Garden Sunflower Quilt Applique Templates
Sunflower Ⓓ

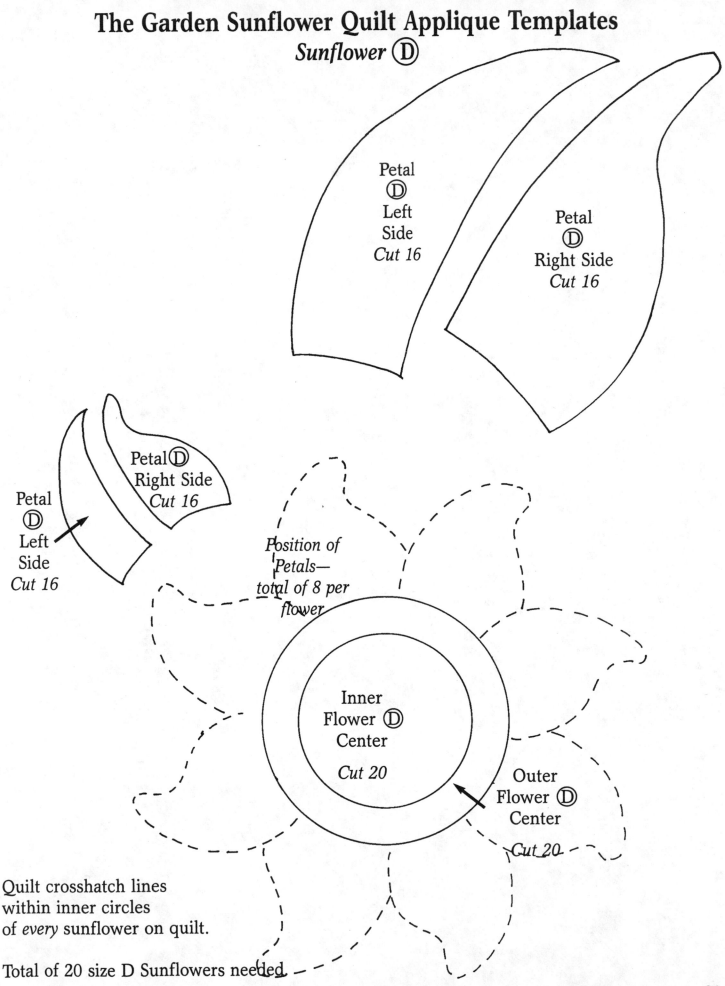

Petal
Ⓓ
Left
Side
Cut 16

Petal
Ⓓ
Right Side
Cut 16

Petal Ⓓ
Right Side
Cut 16

Petal
Ⓓ
Left
Side
Cut 16

*Position of
Petals—
total of 8 per
flower*

Inner
Flower Ⓓ
Center

Cut 20

Outer
Flower Ⓓ
Center

Cut 20

Quilt crosshatch lines
within inner circles
of *every* sunflower on quilt.

Total of 20 size D Sunflowers needed.

The Garden Sunflower Quilt Applique Layout
Center Watering Can Patch

Cut along dotted line.

G

W

D

To create the Center Watering Can Patch layout, match corresponding letters and notches along dotted lines and tape together.

Completed Applique layout will look like this.

Note: The Watering Can in the center, is quilted. Quilting Templates for it begin on page 35.

The Garden Sunflower Quilt Applique Layout
Center Watering Can Patch

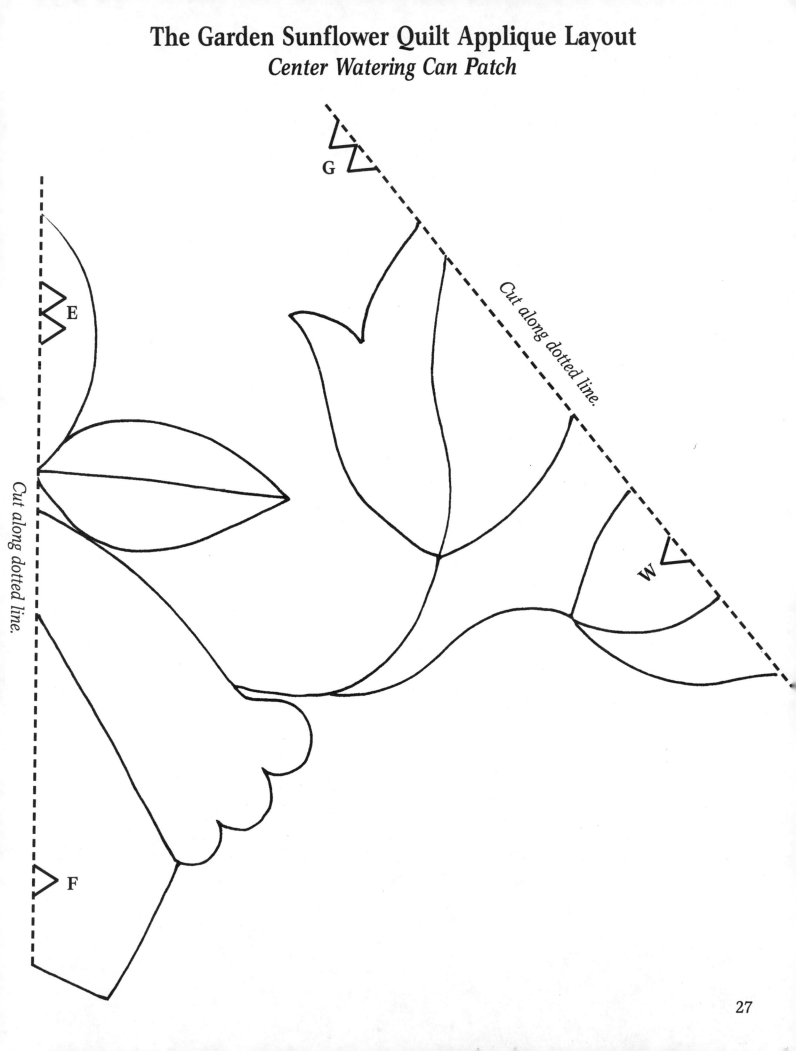

G

E

Cut along dotted line.

Cut along dotted line.

W

F

The Garden Sunflower Quilt Applique Layout
Center Watering Can Patch

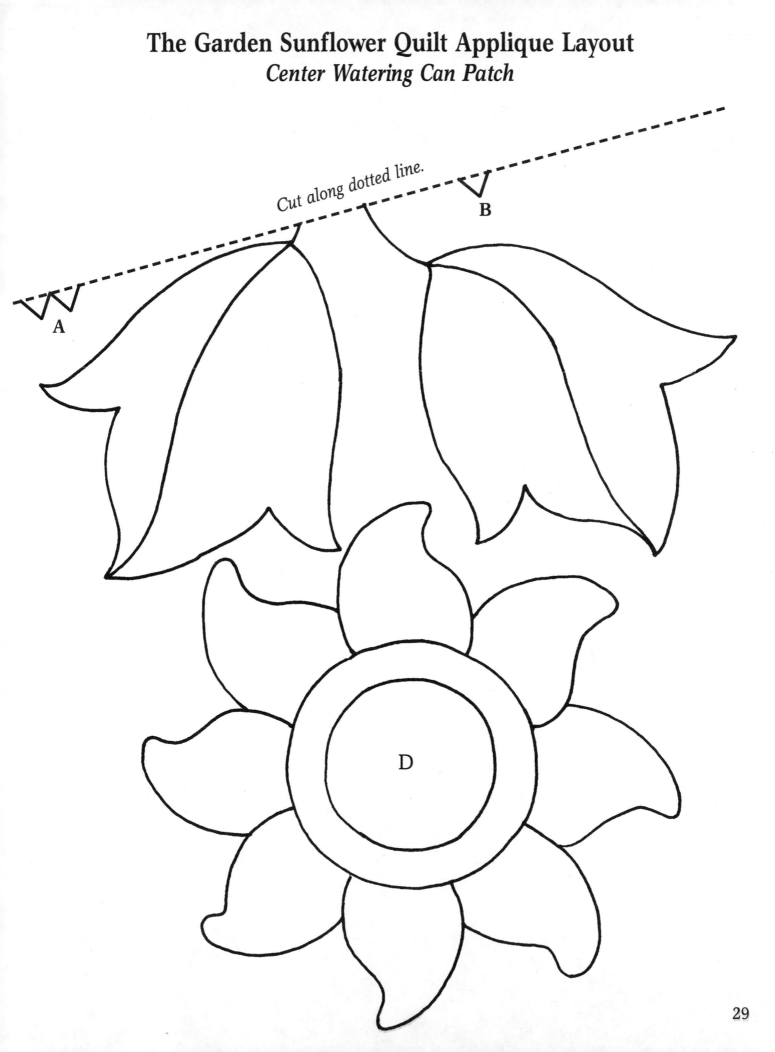

The Garden Sunflower Quilt Applique Layout
Center Watering Can Patch

Cut along dotted line.

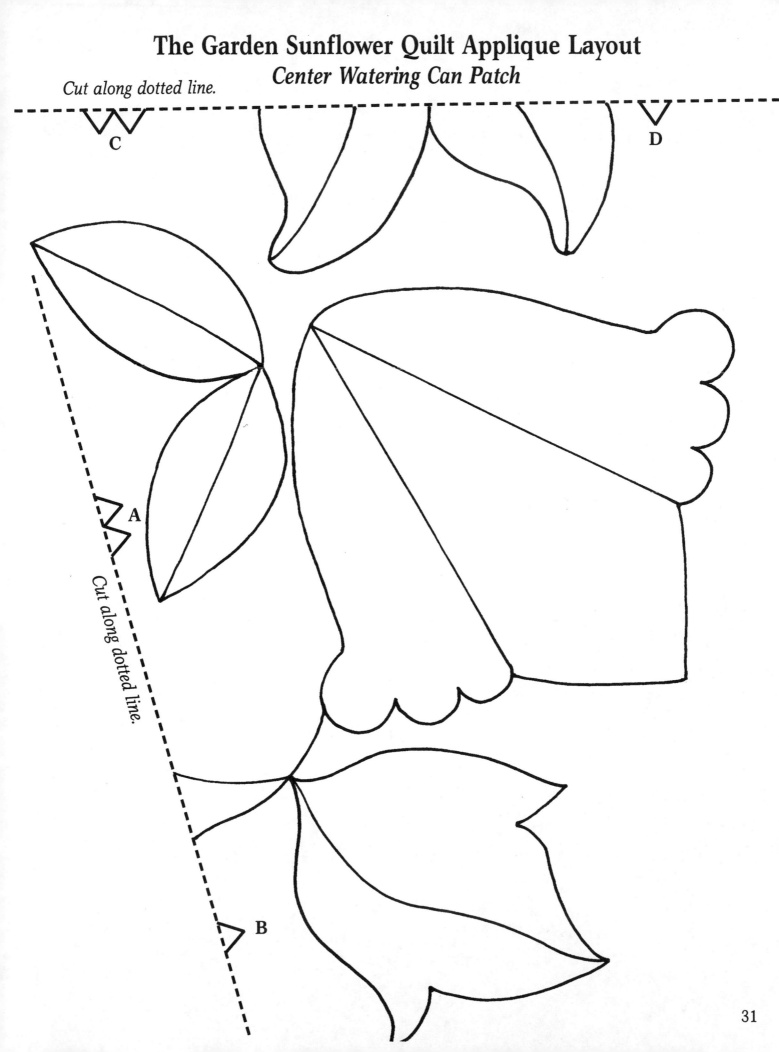

The Garden Sunflower Quilt Applique Layout
Center Watering Can Patch

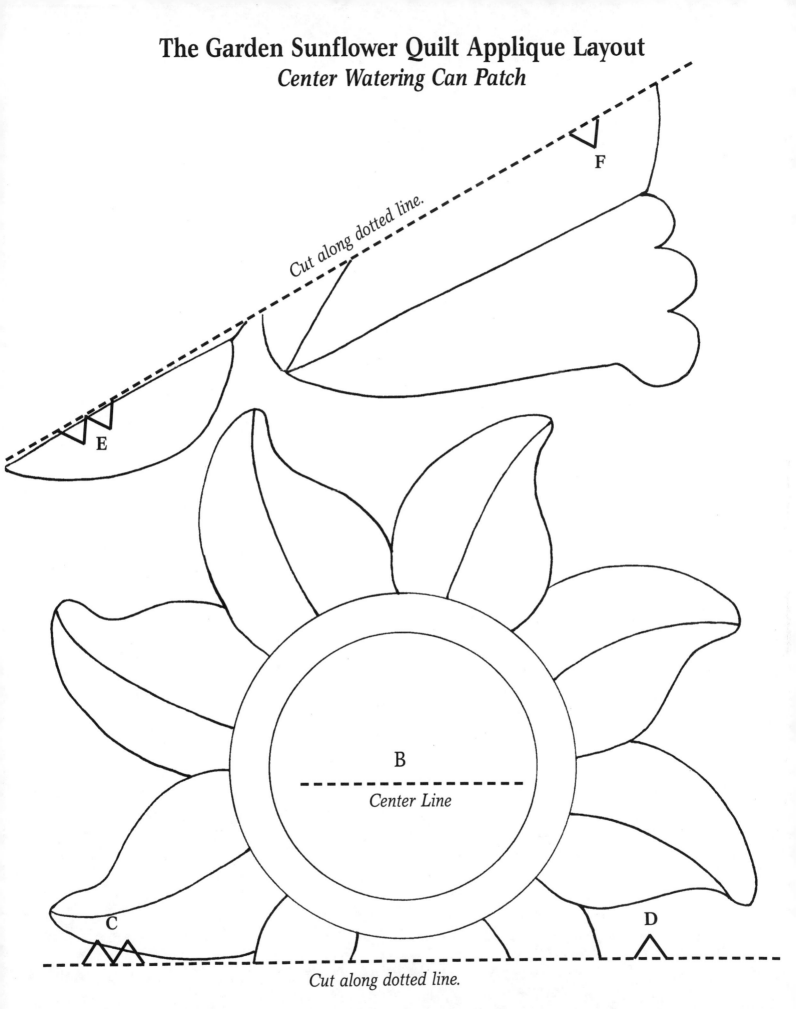

Cut along dotted line.

F

E

B

Center Line

C

D

Cut along dotted line.

The Garden Sunflower Quilt
Quilting Template
Center Watering Can

Connect corresponding letters and notches along dotted lines and tape. Refer to page 25 for position of Quilted Watering Can within the Center Patch.

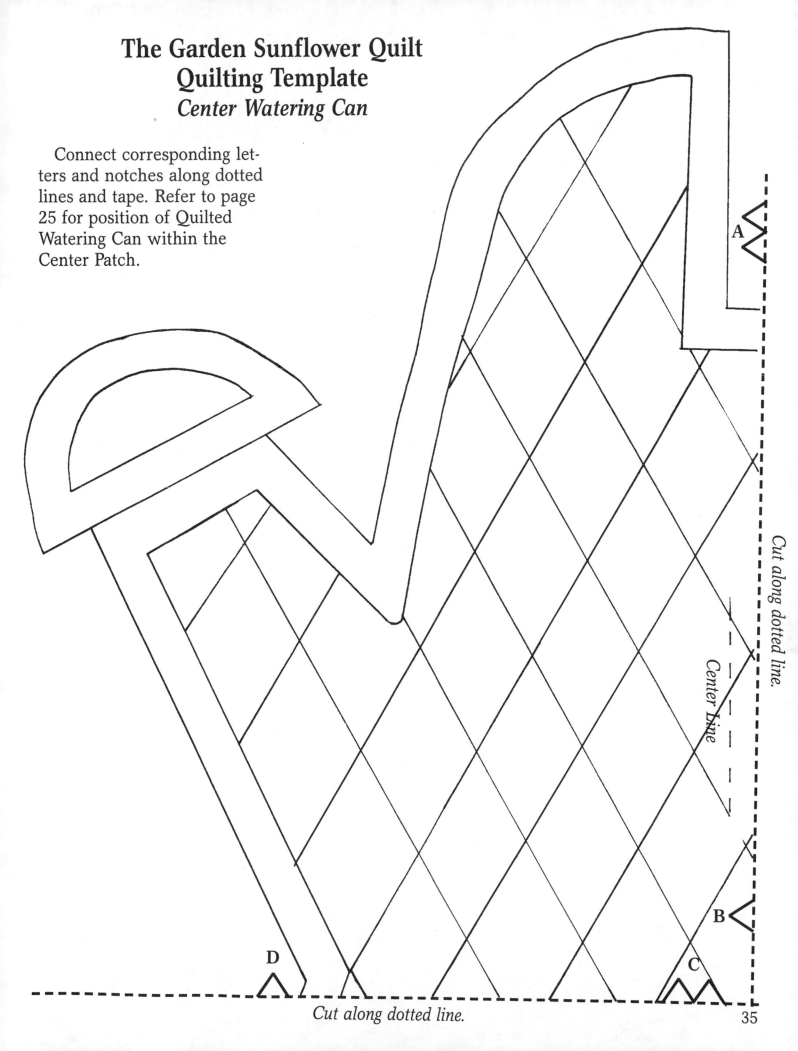

A

Cut along dotted line.

Center Line

B

D

C

Cut along dotted line.

The Garden Sunflower Quilt Quilting Template
Center Watering Can

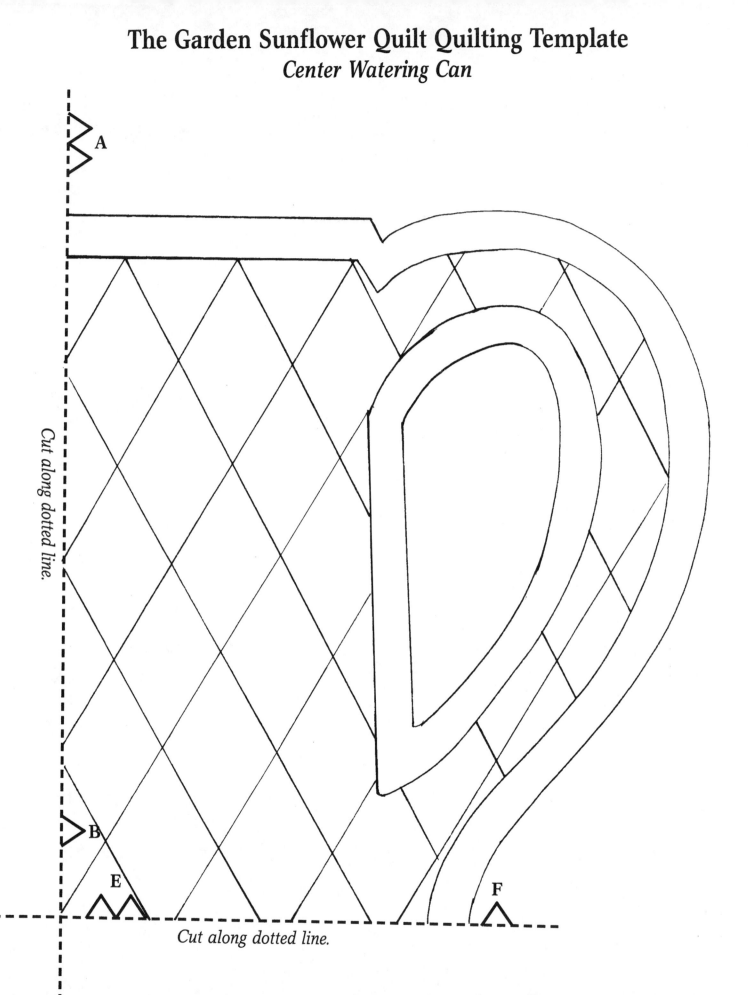

Cut along dotted line.

Cut along dotted line.

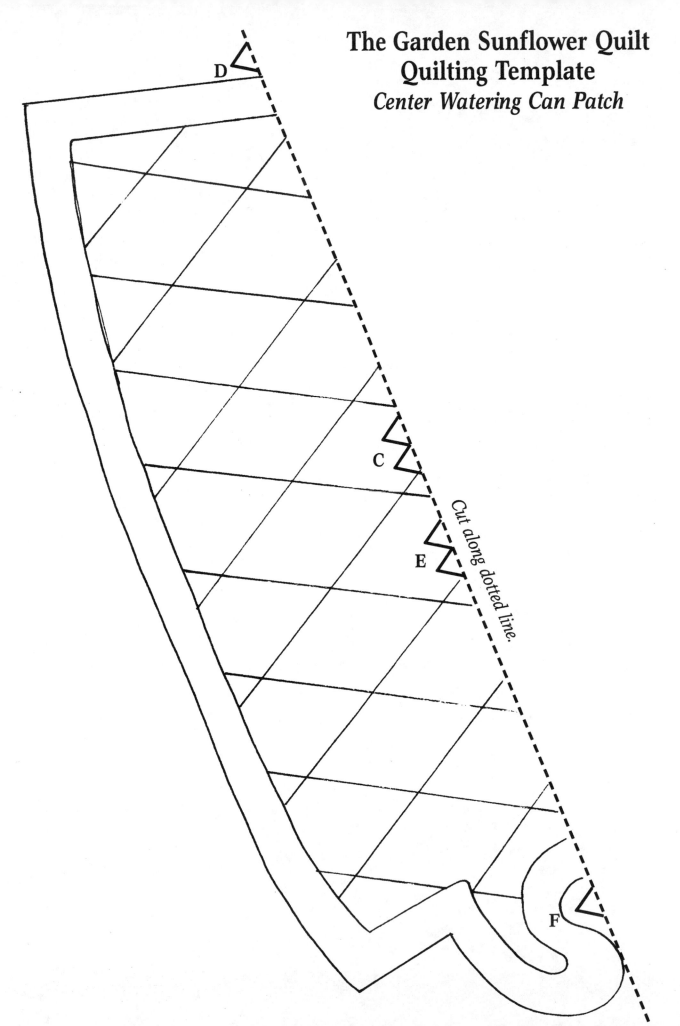

The Garden Sunflower Quilt
Quilting Template
Center Watering Can Patch

D

C

E

Cut along dotted line.

F

The Garden Sunflower Quilt Applique Layout
Single Sunflower Patch

Connect corresponding letters and notches along dotted lines and then tape the pieces together.

Completed layout will look like this:

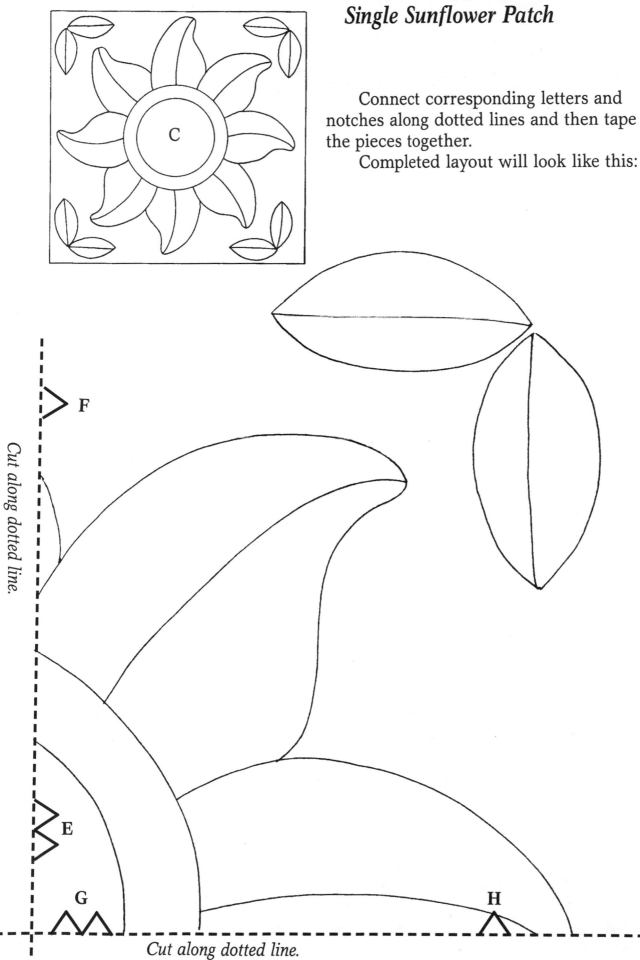

Cut along dotted line.

Cut along dotted line.

The Garden Sunflower Quilt Applique Layout
Single Sunflower Patch

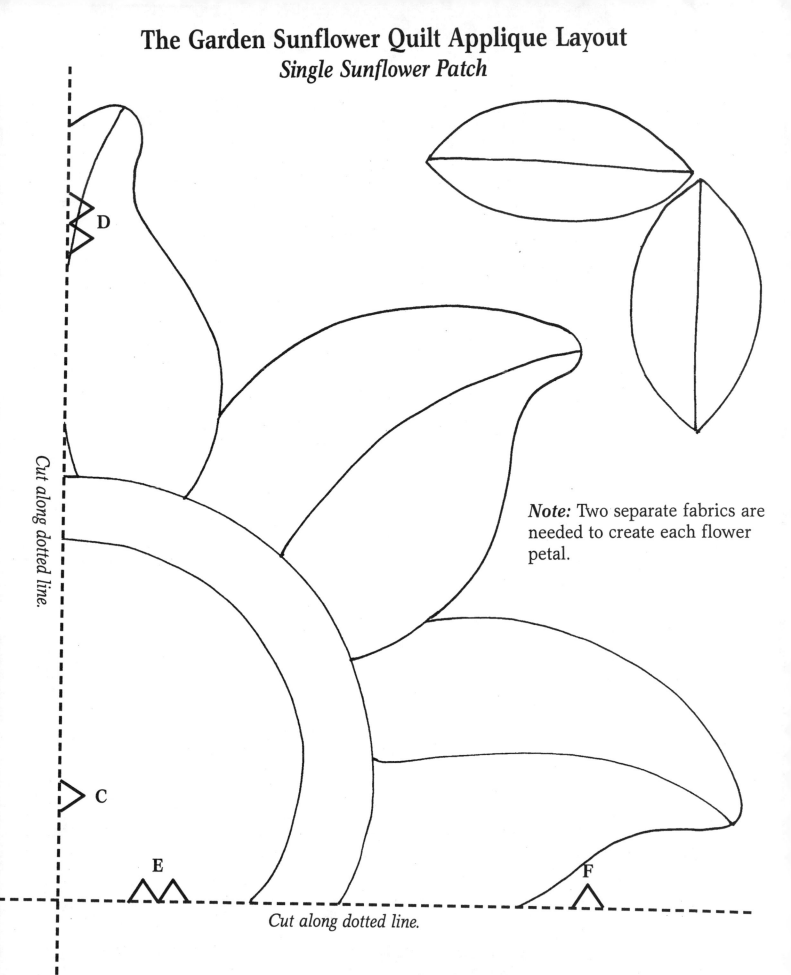

Cut along dotted line.

D

Note: Two separate fabrics are needed to create each flower petal.

C

E

F

Cut along dotted line.

43

The Garden Sunflower Quilt Applique Layout
Single Sunflower Patch

Cut along dotted line.

Cut along dotted line.

45

The Garden Sunflower Quilt Applique Layout
Single Sunflower Patch

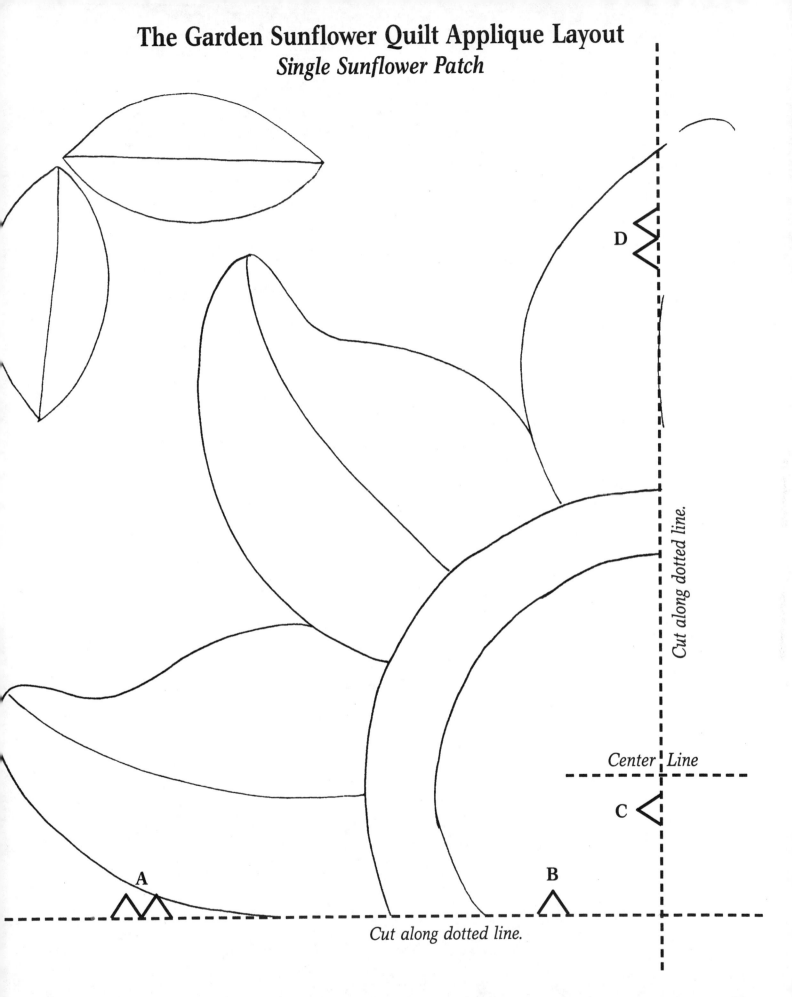

Cut along dotted line.

Center Line

Cut along dotted line.

D

C

A

B

The Garden Sunflower Quilt Applique Layout
Triple Sunflower Patch

Connect corresponding letters and notches along dotted lines and then tape the pieces together.

Completed layout will look like this:

Cut along dotted line.

Cut along dotted line.

The Garden Sunflower Quilt Applique Layout
Triple Sunflower Patch

Cut along dotted line.

F

E

C

D

Cut along dotted line.

The Garden Sunflower Quilt Applique Layout
Triple Sunflower Patch

Cut along dotted line.

Cut along dotted line.

The Garden Sunflower Quilt Quilting Template
Triple Sunflower Patch

Cut along dotted line.

H

G

Center Line

B

Cut along dotted line.

A

The Garden Sunflower Quilt Applique Layout
Envelope-Shaped Pillow Throw

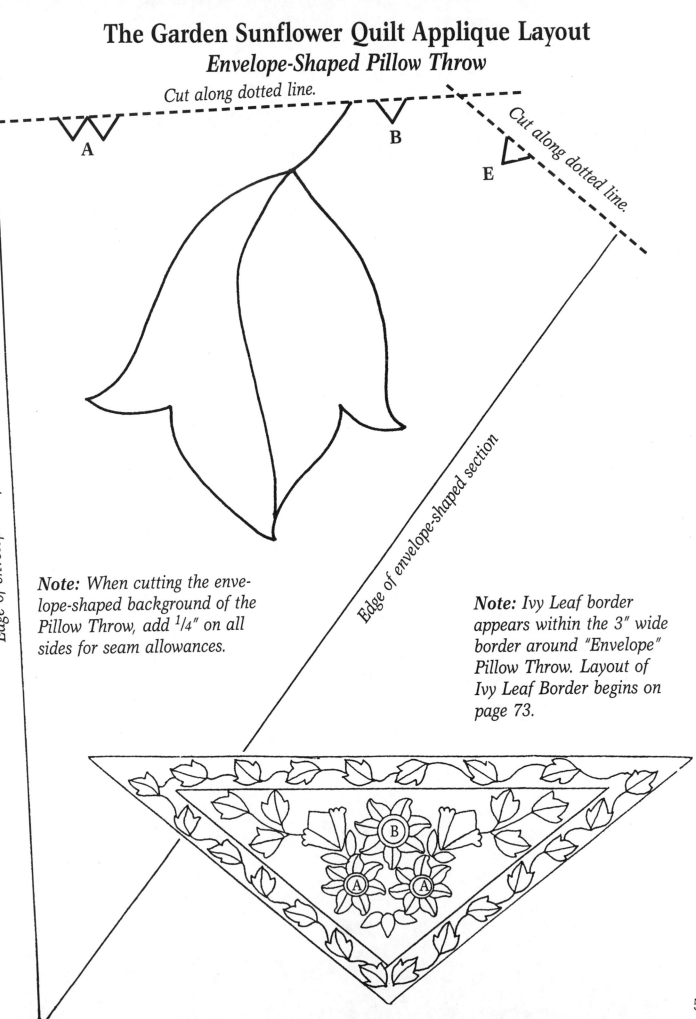

Cut along dotted line.

A

B

E

Cut along dotted line.

Edge of envelope-shaped section

Edge of envelope-shaped section

Note: *When cutting the envelope-shaped background of the Pillow Throw, add $1/4$" on all sides for seam allowances.*

Note: *Ivy Leaf border appears within the 3" wide border around "Envelope" Pillow Throw. Layout of Ivy Leaf Border begins on page 73.*

The Garden Sunflower Quilt Applique Layout
Envelope-Shaped Pillow Throw

Cut along dotted line.

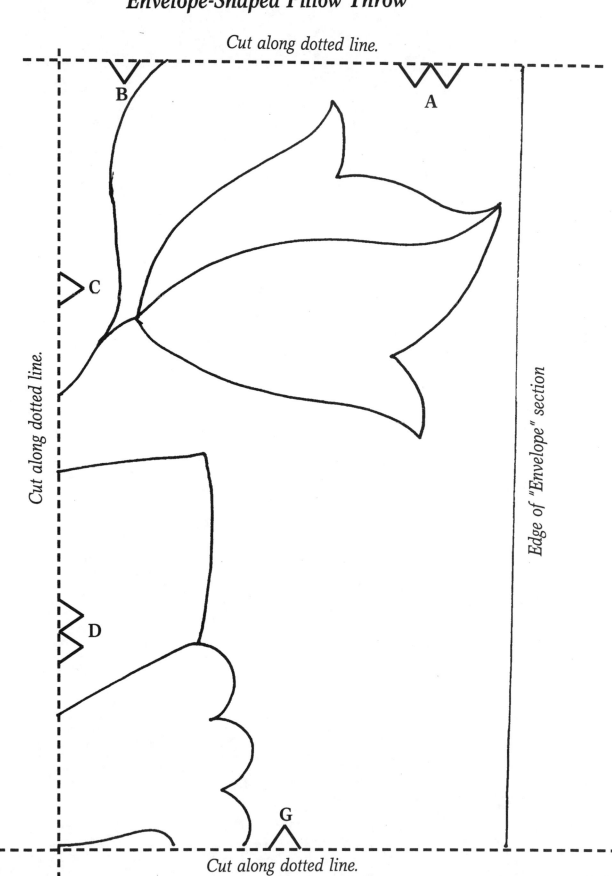

Cut along dotted line.

Cut along dotted line.

Edge of "Envelope" section

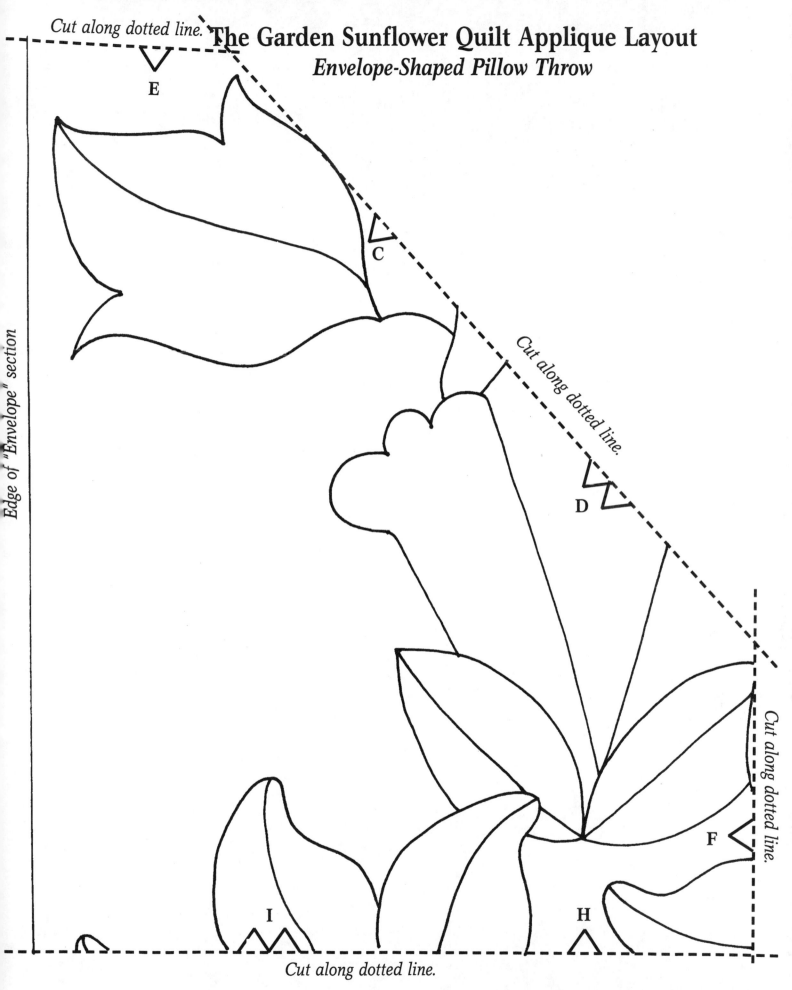

Cut along dotted line.

E

C

Edge of "Envelope" section

Cut along dotted line.

D

Cut along dotted line.

F

I

H

Cut along dotted line.

The Garden Sunflower Quilt Applique Layout
Envelope-Shaped Pillow Throw

Edge of "Envelope" section

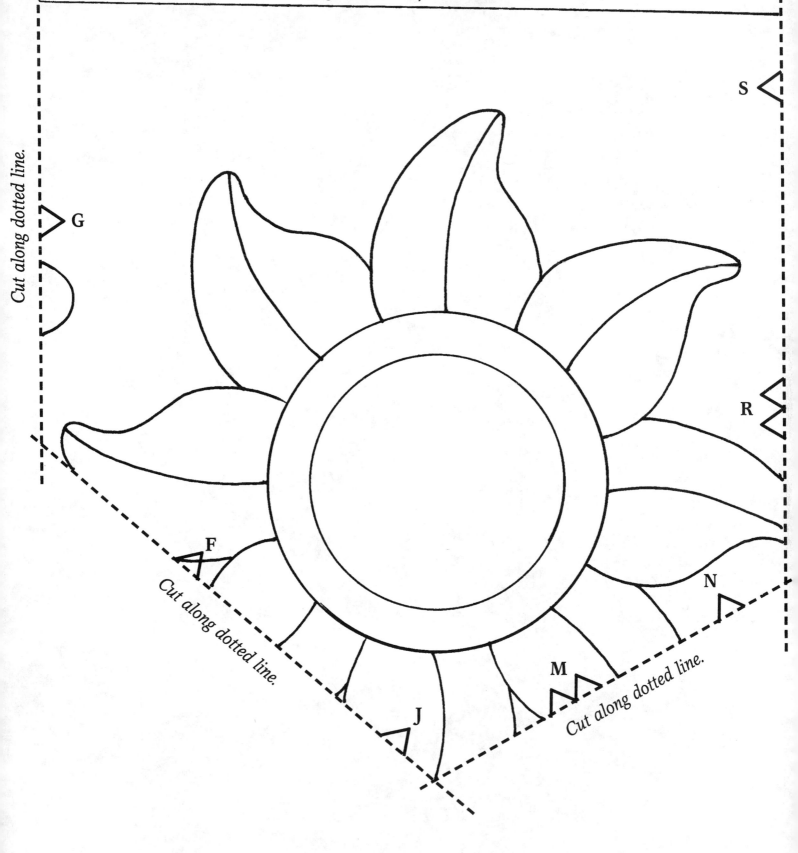

Cut along dotted line.

G

S

R

Cut along dotted line.

F

J

M

N

Cut along dotted line.

Cut along dotted line.

I

H

J

Edge of "Envelope" section

K

Cut along dotted line.

Center Line

Edge of "Envelope" section

L

The Garden Sunflower Quilt Applique Layout
Envelope-Shaped Pillow Throw

Cut along dotted line.

Cut along dotted line.

Cut along dotted line.

Edge of "Envelope" section

Q

T

U

P

O

N

M

K

L

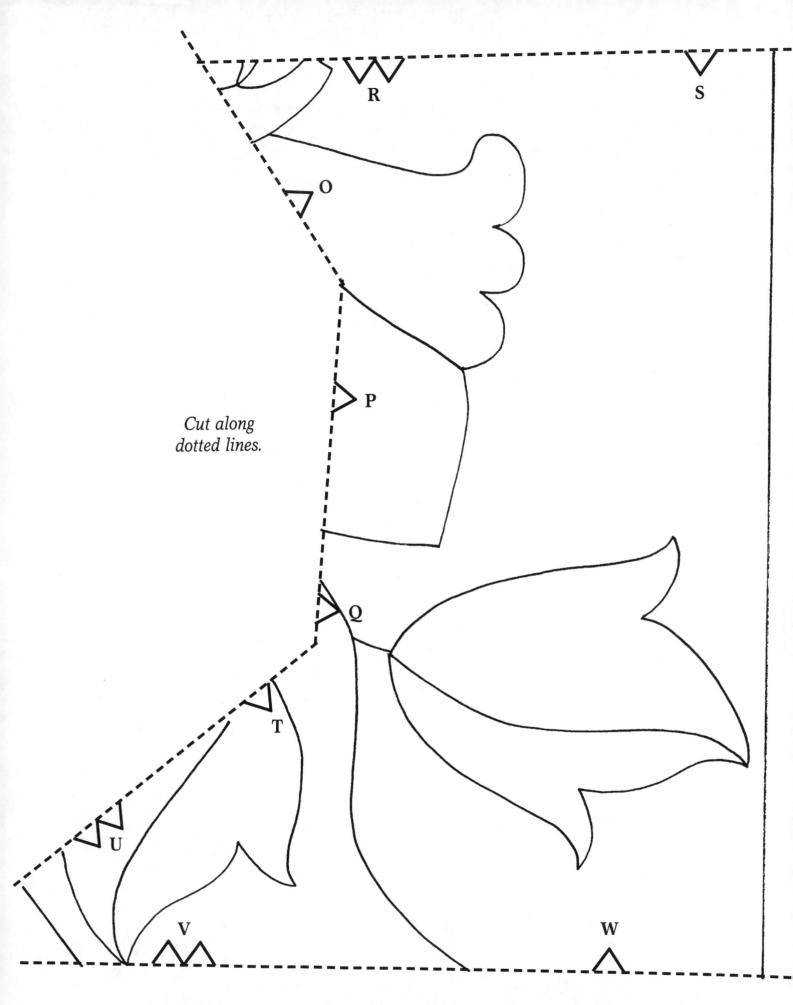

Cut along dotted lines.

R

S

O

P

Q

T

U

V

W

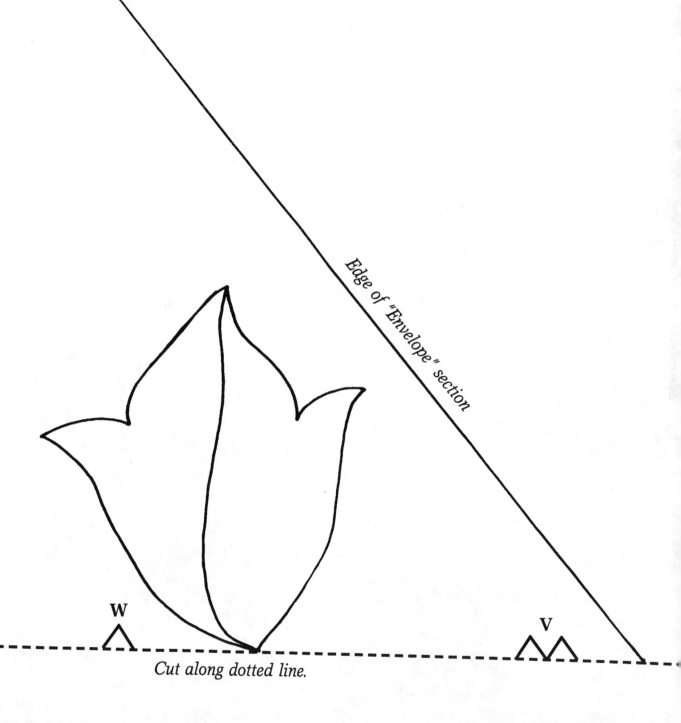

Edge of "Envelope" section

Edge of "Envelope" section

W

V

Cut along dotted line.

The Garden Sunflower Quilt Applique Layout
Ivy Border

Cut along dotted line.

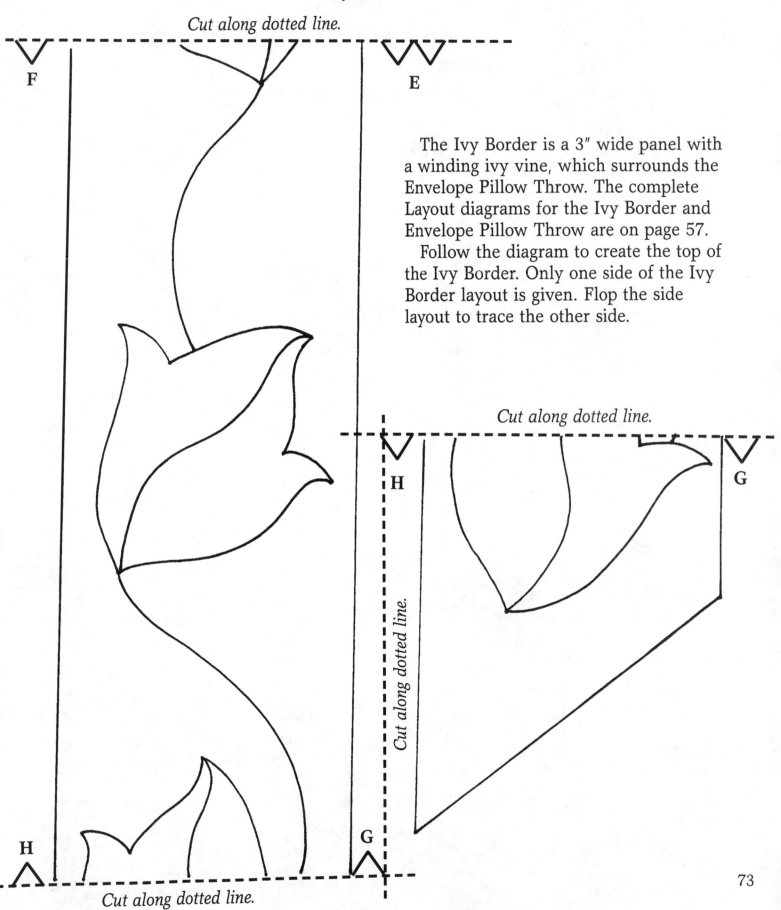

The Ivy Border is a 3″ wide panel with a winding ivy vine, which surrounds the Envelope Pillow Throw. The complete Layout diagrams for the Ivy Border and Envelope Pillow Throw are on page 57.

Follow the diagram to create the top of the Ivy Border. Only one side of the Ivy Border layout is given. Flop the side layout to trace the other side.

Cut along dotted line.

Cut along dotted line.

Cut along dotted line.

The Garden Sunflower Quilt Applique Layout
Ivy Border

Cut along dotted line.

Cut along dotted line.

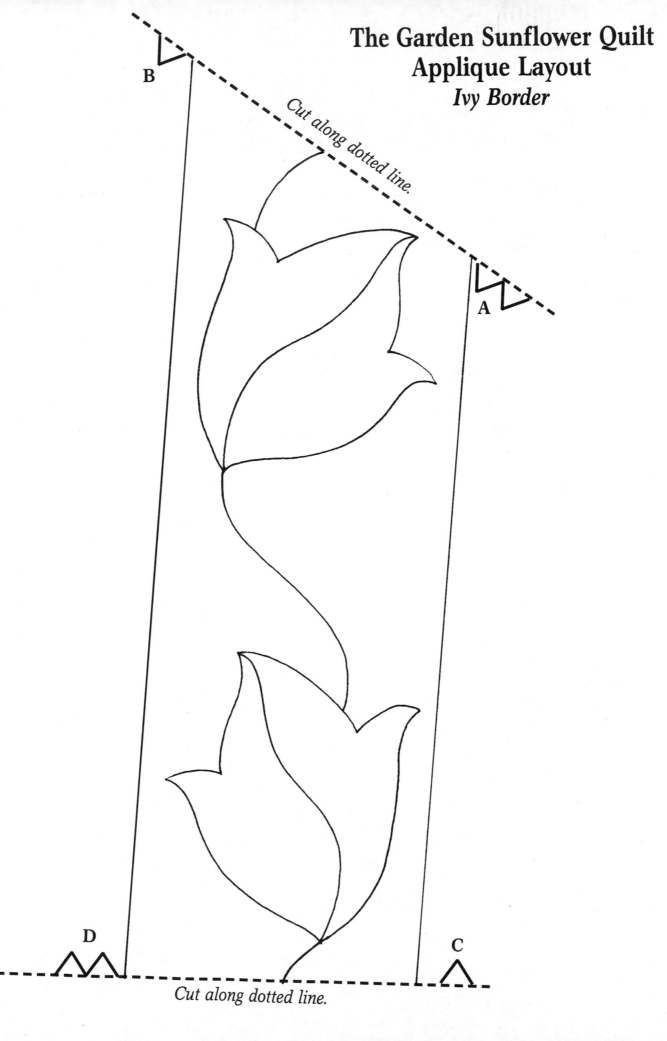

B

Cut along dotted line.

A

D

C

Cut along dotted line.

The Garden Sunflower Quilt Applique Layout
Ivy Border

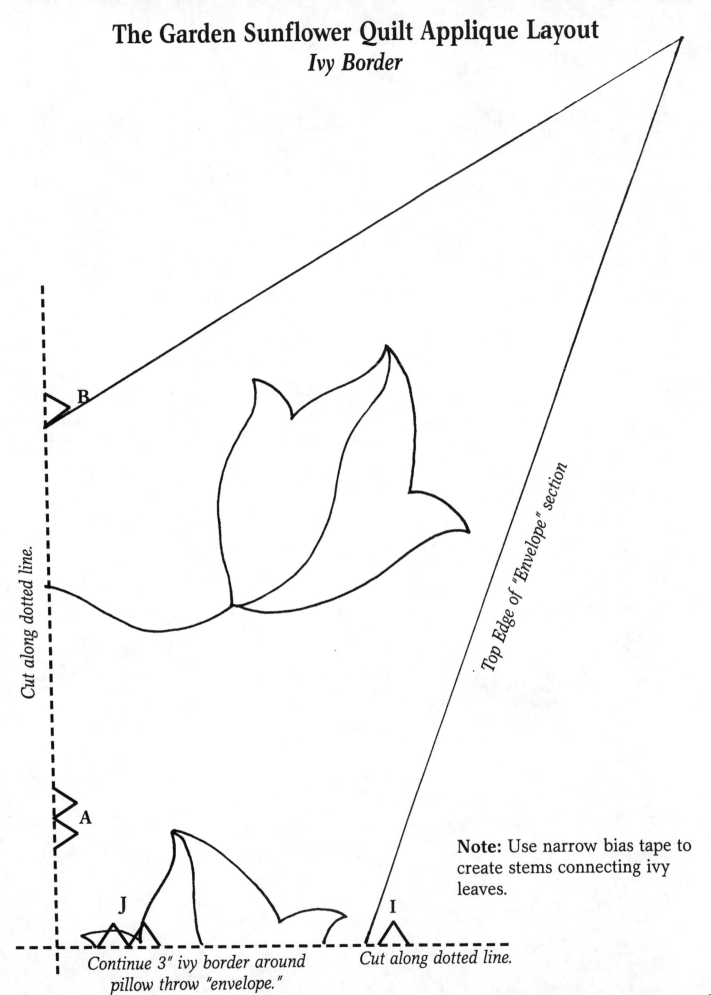

B

A

Cut along dotted line.

Top Edge of "Envelope" section

Note: Use narrow bias tape to create stems connecting ivy leaves.

J

I

Continue 3" ivy border around pillow throw "envelope."

Cut along dotted line.

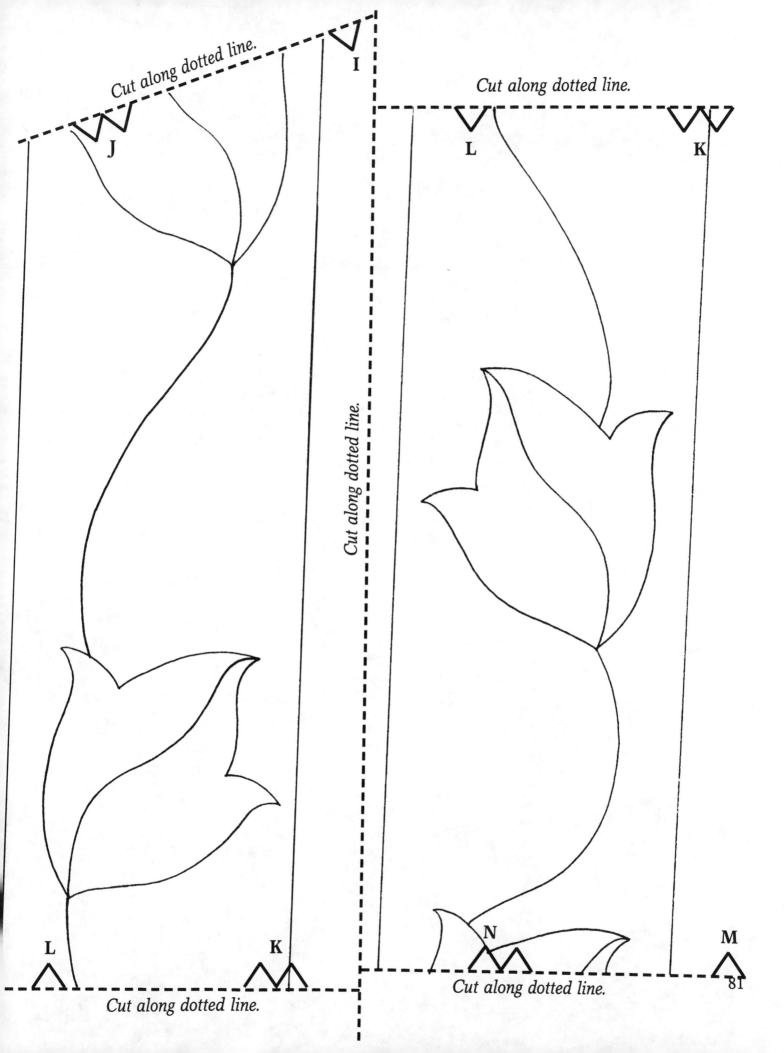

Cut along dotted line.

I

Cut along dotted line.

J

Cut along dotted line.

L

K

L

K

N

M

Cut along dotted line.

Cut along dotted line.

81

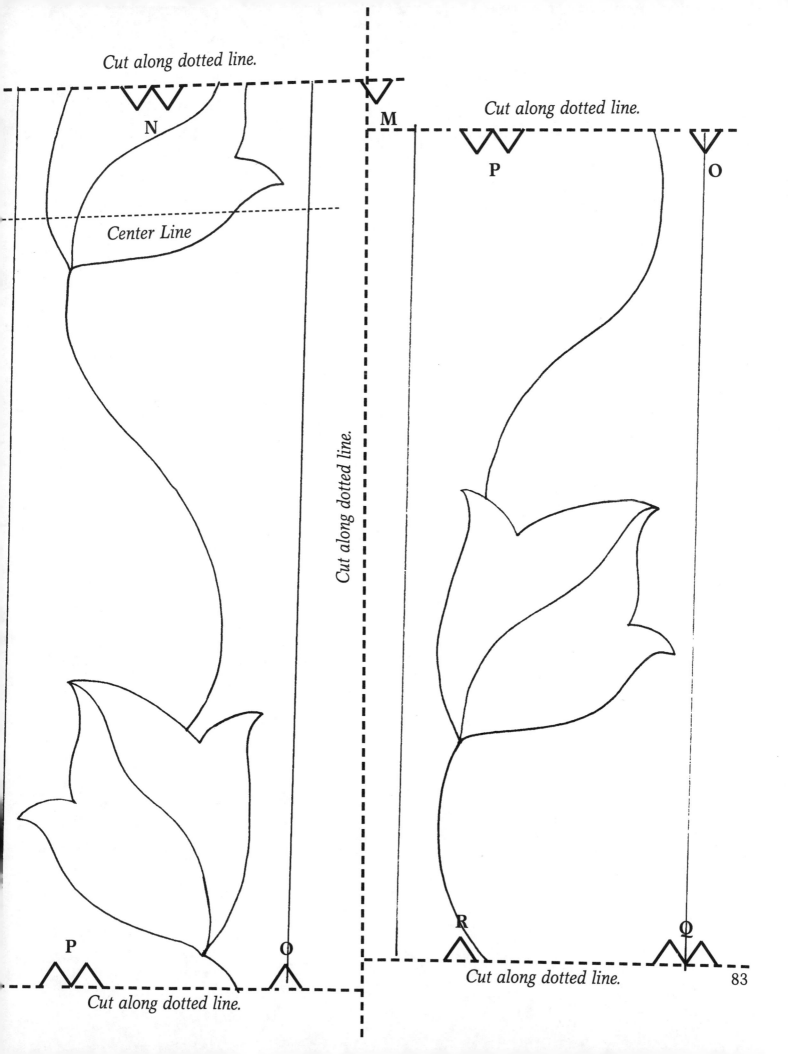

Cut along dotted line.

N

Center Line

Cut along dotted line.

M

Cut along dotted line.

P

O

P

O

P

O

R

Q

Cut along dotted line.

Cut along dotted line.

83

The Garden Sunflower Quilt
Applique Layout
Ivy Border

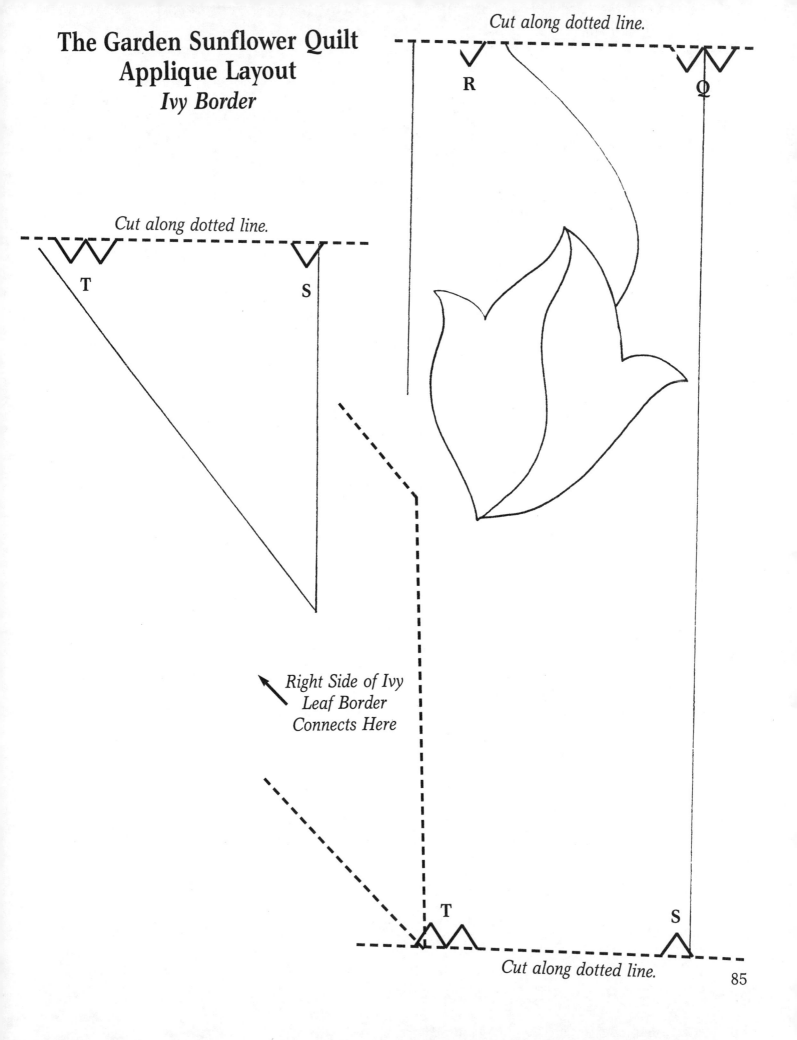

Cut along dotted line.

Cut along dotted line.

R

Q

Cut along dotted line.

T

S

*Right Side of Ivy
Leaf Border
Connects Here*

T

S

Cut along dotted line.

85

The Garden Sunflower Quilt Applique Template
Notched Border

To create the Corner Border/Side Border layout, connect corresponding letters and notches along dotted lines and then tape the pieces together.

The complete layout will look like this:

Sunflower D

Cut along dotted line.

Cut along dotted line.

D

C

A

B

Edge of Quilt

The Garden Sunflower Quilt Applique Template
Notched Border

Top of Quilt

G

H

D

E

F

Cut along dotted line.

The Garden Sunflower Quilt Applique Template
Notched Border

Cut along dotted line.

A

D

B

Edge of Quilt

The Garden Sunflower Quilt Applique Template
Notched Border

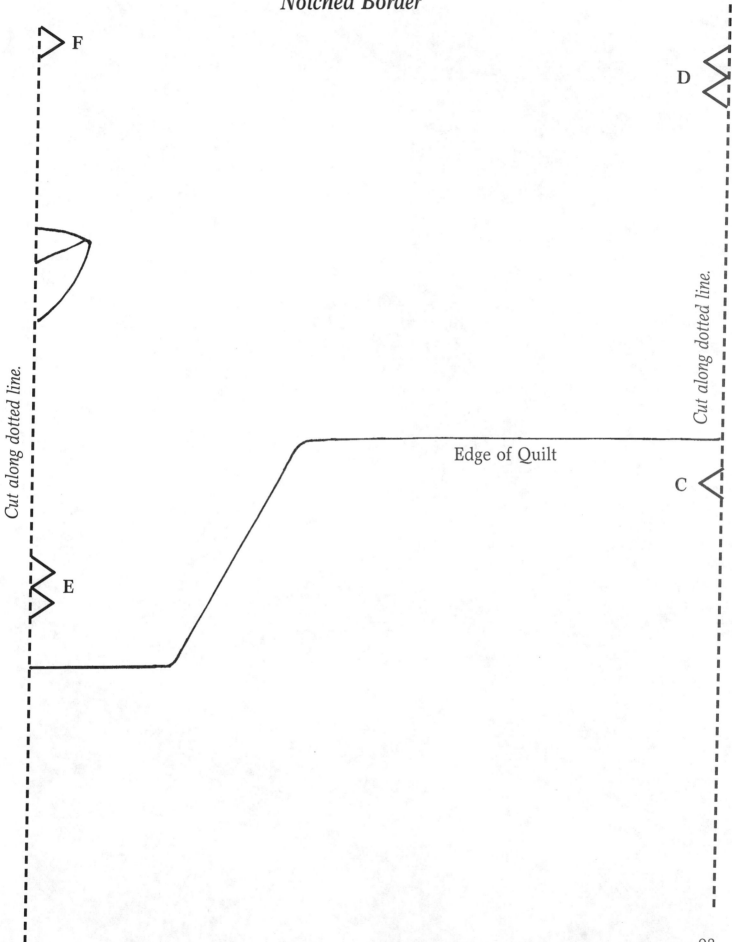

F

D

Cut along dotted line.

Cut along dotted line.

Edge of Quilt

C

E

The Garden Sunflower Quilt Applique Layout
Corner Border/Side Border

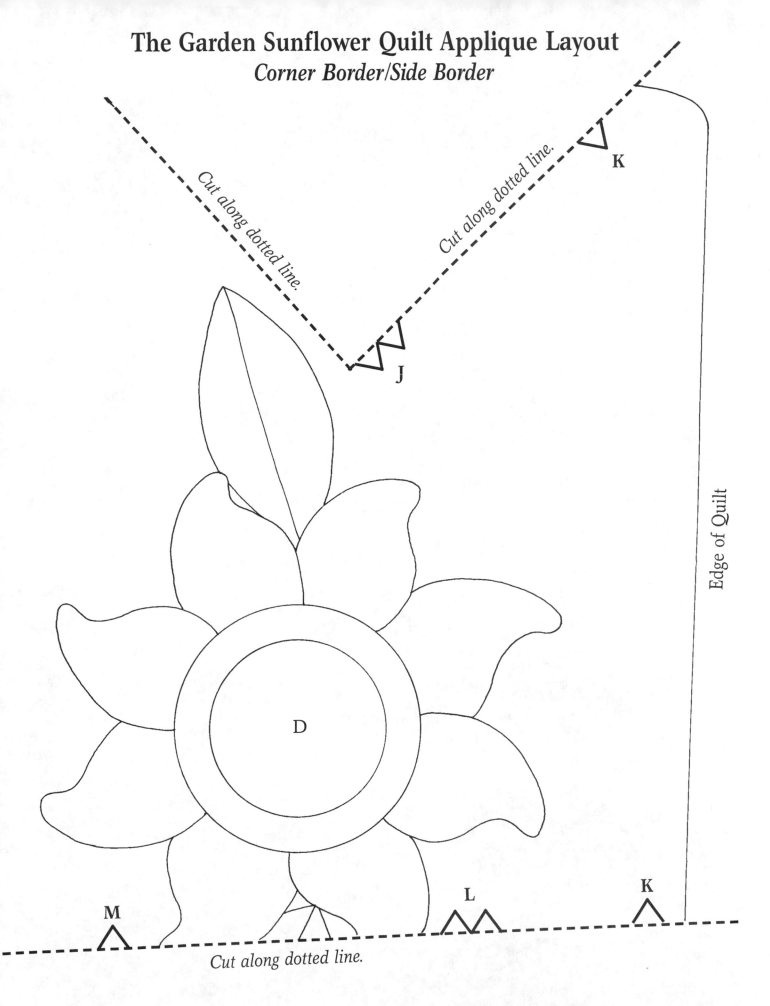

Cut along dotted line.

Cut along dotted line.

K

Cut along dotted line.

J

Edge of Quilt

D

M

L

K

The Garden Sunflower Quilt Applique Layout
Corner Border/Side Border

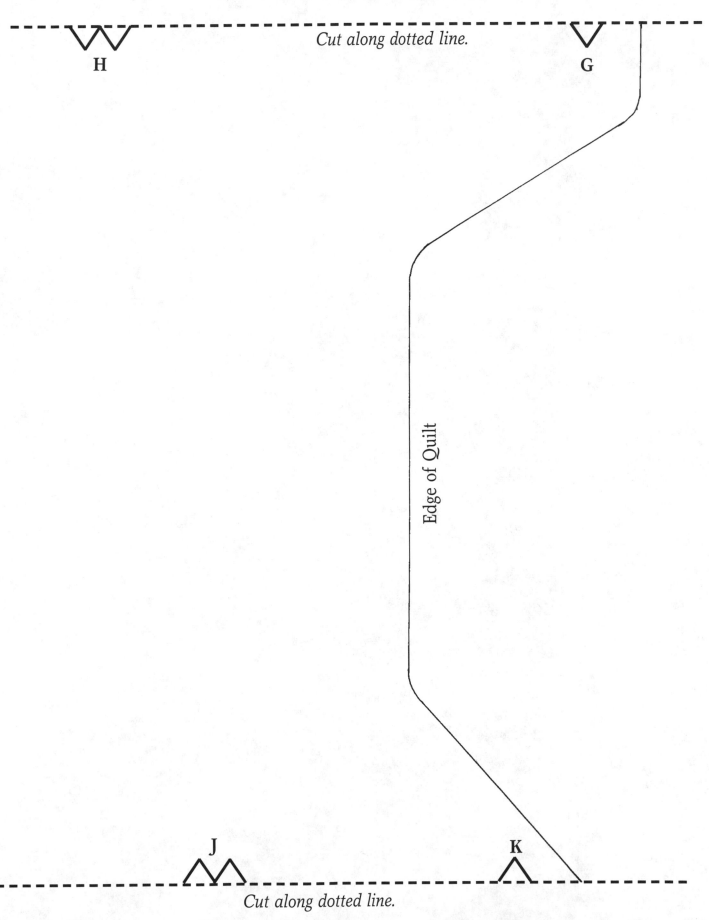

Cut along dotted line.

H

G

Edge of Quilt

J

K

Cut along dotted line.

The Garden Sunflower Quilt Applique Layout
Corner Border/Side Border

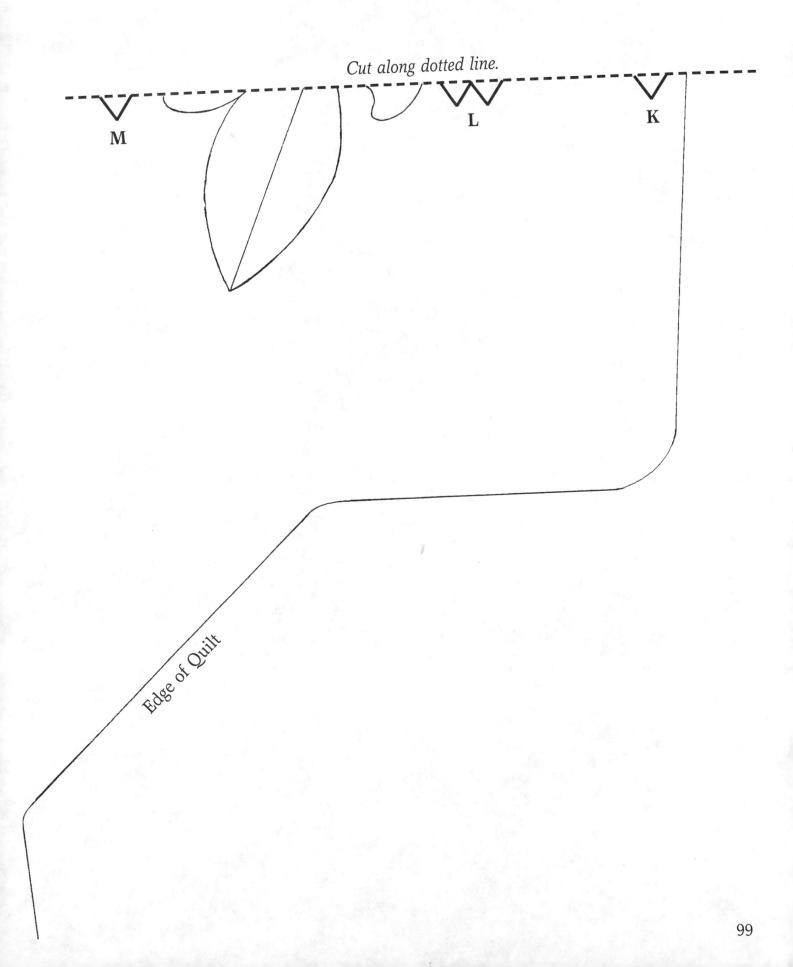

Cut along dotted line.

M

L

K

Edge of Quilt

The Garden Sunflower Quilting Layout
Border of Swirls

Cut along dotted line.

Connect corresponding letters and notches to complete this quilting template.

The Quilted Border of Swirls appears within the 5″ panel at the base of the Pillow Throw section.

Connect the corresponding letters and notches to complete the quilting template.

The Garden Sunflower Quilting Layout
Border of Swirls

B △

A △△

Cut along dotted line.

Order Form

(all books are paperback)

Quantity		Price	Total
_____	The Country Bride Quilt	$12.95	$_____
_____	The Country Bride Quilt Collection	$12.95	$_____
_____	The Country Lily Quilt	$12.95	$_____
_____	The Country Love Quilt	$12.95	$_____
_____	The Country Paradise Quilt	$12.95	$_____
_____	The Country Songbird Quilt	$12.95	$_____
_____	Country Quilts for Children	$12.95	$_____
_____	The Country Tea Rose Quilt	$12.95	$_____
_____	The Garden Sunflower Quilt	$14.95	$_____
_____	The Heart of Roses Quilt	$14.95	$_____
_____	Making Animal Quilts	$12.95	$_____
_____	Patterns for Making Amish Dolls	$12.95	$_____
_____	Amish Quilt Patterns	$12.95	$_____
_____	Small Amish Quilt Patterns	$12.95	$_____
_____	Favorite Applique Patterns from The Old Country Store, Vol. 1	$15.95	$_____
_____	Favorite Applique Patterns from The Old Country Store, Vol. 2	$15.95	$_____
_____	Favorite Applique Patterns from The Old Country Store, Vol. 3	$15.95	$_____
_____	Favorite Applique Patterns from The Old Country Store, Vol. 4	$15.95	$_____
_____	Favorite Applique Patterns for the Holidays from The Old Country Store, Vol. 5	$15.95	$_____
_____	Favorite Applique Patterns from The Old Country Store—Country Critters, Vol. 6	$15.95	$_____

Subtotal _____

PA residents add 6% sales tax _____

Shipping and handling (Add 10%, $2.50 minimum) _____

TOTAL _____

METHOD OF PAYMENT

☐ Check or Money Order *(payable to Good Books in U.S. funds)*

☐ Please charge my:
  ☐ MasterCard ☐ Visa

\# _____ exp. date _____

Signature _____

Name _____

Name _____

Address _____

City _____ State _____ Zip _____

Telephone (_____) _____

SHIP TO: *(if different)*

Name _____

Address _____

City _____ State _____ Zip _____

Telephone (_____) _____

Mail order to:

Good Books®

PO Box 419, Intercourse, PA 17534

Or call 800/762-7171 (in Canada, call collect 717/768-7171)

(Prices subject to change without notice.)

About The Old Country Store

Cheryl A. Benner and Rachel T. Pellman are
associated with The Old Country Store, located
along Route 340 in Intercourse, Pennsylvania.
The Store offers crafts from more than 300 arti-
sans, most of whom are local Amish and
Mennonites. There are quilts of traditional and
contemporary designs, patchwork pillows and
pillow kits, afghans, stuffed animals, dolls,
tablecloths, and Christmas tree ornaments.
Other handcrafted items include potholders,
sunbonnets, and wooden toys.

For the do-it-yourself quilter, the Store offers
quilt supplies, fabric at discount prices, and a
large selection of quilt books and patterns.

Located on the second floor of the Store is The
People's Place Quilt Museum. The Museum,
which opened in 1988, features antique Amish
quilts and crib quilts, as well as a small collection of dolls, doll quilts, socks, and other decorative arts.

The People's Place Quilt Museum

Cheryl A. Benner

Rachel T. Pellman

About the Authors

Cheryl A. Benner and Rachel T. Pellman together developed the book, *The Garden Sunflower Quilt.* Benner created the patterns; then together they selected the fabrics and supervised the making of the original quilt by Lancaster County Mennonite women. This is Benner's and Pellman's eighth collaboration on quilt designs with related books. Their earlier books are the popular *The Country Love Quilt, The Country Lily Quilt, The Country Songbird Quilt, The Country Bride Quilt Collection, The Country Paradise Quilt, The Country Tea Rose Quilt,* and *Favorite Applique Patterns from the Old Country Store, Volumes 1 through 6.* Benner and Pellman also work together to design original fabrics for The Old Country Store, released nationally by Springs Industries.

Benner, her husband Lamar, and two young sons live near Lancaster, Pennsylvania. She is a graduate of the Art Institute of Philadelphia (PA). Benner is the children's book illustrator of *The Boy and the Quilt, Applesauce, Birthday Chickens,* and *Amos and Susie: An Amish Story,* as well as two coloring books, *An Amish Quilt and An Amish Farm.*

Pellman lives near Lancaster, Pennsylvania, with her husband Kenneth and their two sons. She is co-author of *The Country Bride Quilt. She is also the author of Tips for Quilters, Amish Quilt Patterns,* and *Small Amish Quilt Patterns;* co-author with Jan Steffy of *Patterns for Making Amish Dolls and Doll Clothes;* and co-author with her husband Kenneth of *A Treasury of Amish Quilts, The World of Amish Quilts, Amish Crib Quilts,* and *Amish Doll Quilts, Dolls and Other Playthings.*